BRIGHT STARS

of

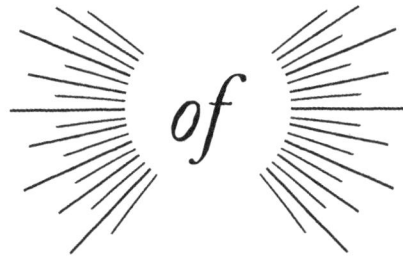

BLACK BRITISH HISTORY

This book is dedicated to my children, Felix and Frankie, to my husband Richard, and to the memory of my mother Margaret and my father John, stars who shine on eternally in my heart. – JTW

My love and gratitude to Joel, Reuben and Sebastian, for the light you bring to my life. – AV

First published in the United Kingdom in 2023 by
Thames & Hudson Ltd, 6-24 Britannia Street, London, WC1X 9JD

This paperback edition published in 2025

Bright Stars of Black British History © 2023 Thames & Hudson Ltd, London
Text © 2023 Joanna Brown
Illustrations © 2023 Angela Vives

EU Authorized Representative: Interart S.A.R.L.
19 rue Charles Auray, 93500 Pantin, Paris, France
productsafety@thameshudson.co.uk
interart.fr

A CIP catalogue record for this book is available from the British Library

ISBN 978-0-500-66044-7
01

Printed in China by Shenzen Reliance Printing Co. Ltd

FSC
www.fsc.org
MIX
Paper | Supporting
responsible forestry
FSC® C102842

Be the first to know about our new releases,
exclusive content and author events by visiting
thamesandhudson.com
thamesandhudsonusa.com
thamesandhudson.com.au

J.T. WILLIAMS

BRIGHT STARS

of

BLACK BRITISH HISTORY

ILLUSTRATED BY ANGELA VIVES

t&h

Contents

Introduction

Did you know that the famous nurse Mary Seacole developed her super nursing skills in Jamaica when she was a girl, practising on dolls and pets before braving the front lines of the Crimea to heal the sick? Have you heard about how the actor Ira Aldridge narrowly escaped capture by slave traders as a boy, before gracing stages all over Europe as one of the greatest ever Shakespearean performers? Have you ever wondered why Claudia Jones, a political journalist, founded Notting Hill Carnival, Britain's legendary celebration of Caribbean culture?

Bright Stars of Black British History is a collection of illustrated biographies shining a light on the lives of Black British people in history. It is a celebration of their contributions to a shared past. The Black presence in Britain is long-standing. People of African descent have lived in Britain for many centuries, and have influenced the course of history in powerful and exciting ways. The stories told here are tightly interwoven with familiar threads in the narrative of British history: the court of King Henry VIII, transatlantic slavery and its abolition, Queen Victoria's reign, the First and Second World Wars, the Jazz Age, and the Windrush story.

Each of the figures in this book has a fascinating story to tell, yet some are just beginning to gain the recognition they deserve. These Bright Stars are people who have made their mark on the course of history because of their courage and their confidence in the possibility of change. By sharing their stories we celebrate them, as the light of their legacies shines brightly to inspire us and give us hope for the future.

When we look up at the night sky, some stars appear to shine more brightly than others. But look closely and you will catch glimpses of other stars in between, stars that join the bright stars together to make up the constellations. There are always people, brave and bold, whose light may be hidden from us, people whose names may not appear in the history books, but whose contribution is key. The difference is simply distance – move closer to a star and it will shine more brightly in your view.

Though we may not always know their names, or the details of their lives, we should also honour the histories of those people who came together as a community to work for change: the rebels and runaways who resisted enslavement; the Sons – and surely Daughters – of Africa who fought for slavery's abolition; the nurses and doctors who broke barriers to care for the nation; the servicemen and women who risked their lives for Britain at war; the musicians, writers and artists whose work has enriched, challenged and changed our thinking.

So join us on a journey of celebration and struggle, resilience and resistance, migration and movement, challenge and change. Join us in joy as we honour these Bright Stars of Black British History.

The Romans
to the Tudors

AFRICAN ROMANS IN BRITAIN

The African presence in Britain is well-established. Thanks to archaeological evidence, we know that since the first century CE, when the Romans conquered Britain, African people have lived, thrived and died here.

Born in present-day Libya, North Africa, the Roman Emperor Septimius Severus came to Britain in CE 208. He lived here for three years before dying in York – then called Eboracum – in 211.

The Aurelian Moors were a cohort of North African soldiers in the Roman army, tasked with guarding Hadrian's Wall along the northern border of England. A stone inscription on a block from the wall, as well as a Roman register of visitors to the area, places them there between the years 253 and 258.

'BEACHY HEAD LADY' AND 'IVORY BANGLE LADY'

New technologies can help archaeologists to work out where someone grew up by examining their bones and teeth. In 2012, new examinations of skeletons excavated decades earlier revealed more evidence of African presence around Britain in the first millennium. For example, 'Beachy Head Lady' was a Sub-Saharan African woman who lived in Eastbourne, Sussex, some time between CE 125 and 145.

'Ivory Bangle Lady' is the name given to a skeleton found in York in 1901, belonging to a mixed-race woman of North African ancestry, believed to have lived in the third century. She was buried in a stone coffin with luxurious grave goods, including black bangles of jet and white bangles of ivory.

MEDIAEVAL AND TUDOR PRESENCES

When the Romans left Britain in the fifth century, the links between Africa and Europe diminished – and with them, to some degree, Britain's African population. However, new archaeological finds continue to reveal evidence of African presences in mediaeval Britain from the eleventh through to the fourteenth century.

In the fifteenth century, the sailing of new sea routes opened up direct pathways between Africa and Europe. Recently discovered parish records dating back to the fifteenth and sixteenth centuries place hundreds of Africans living in England: a significant population of Black Tudors in Britain.

John Blanke
(active from 1507)

A TALENTED TRUMPETER
AT THE TUDOR COURT

John Blanke, an African musician, was a star trumpet player at the Tudor court. His name appears in royal records and his painted image graces a famous Tudor scroll: the Westminster Tournament Roll.

Spain, Portugal and Italy were home to many Africans in the sixteenth century, with over 150,000 African people living in Southern Europe by 1521. John may have travelled from Spain to England with the court of Katherine of Aragon in 1501, when she came to marry Prince Arthur.

Arthur was the son of Henry VII, and heir to the English throne.
As Katherine travelled, she was accompanied by an impressive retinue
worthy of a queen. Around sixty court servants and musicians arrived
at Plymouth, and together they made their way to London. The royal
wedding took place as planned, but Arthur died just five months later
of sweating sickness. What did the future hold for the young widow?
Katherine and her court remained in England while arrangements
for a new marriage were discussed.

Music was key to Tudor court life. Learning to sing, dance and play instruments – such as the viol or the virginals, the lute or recorder – was considered an essential cultural accomplishment for members of the royal family and their courtiers. Music was played at pageants and masqued performances, at ceremonial tournaments and jousting matches. Song was woven through religious worship.

Trumpet players were employed as messengers as well as musicians. Their fantastic fanfares announced births, marriages and deaths of members of the royal household. Their grand flourishes sounded at feasts, heralding royal entrances and exits.

A note of wages paid to 'John Blanke the blacke trumpet' on 7 December 1507 is John's first appearance in the historical record. He was one of eight trumpeters in the royal court of King Henry VII, father of both the late Prince Arthur and the future King Henry VIII.

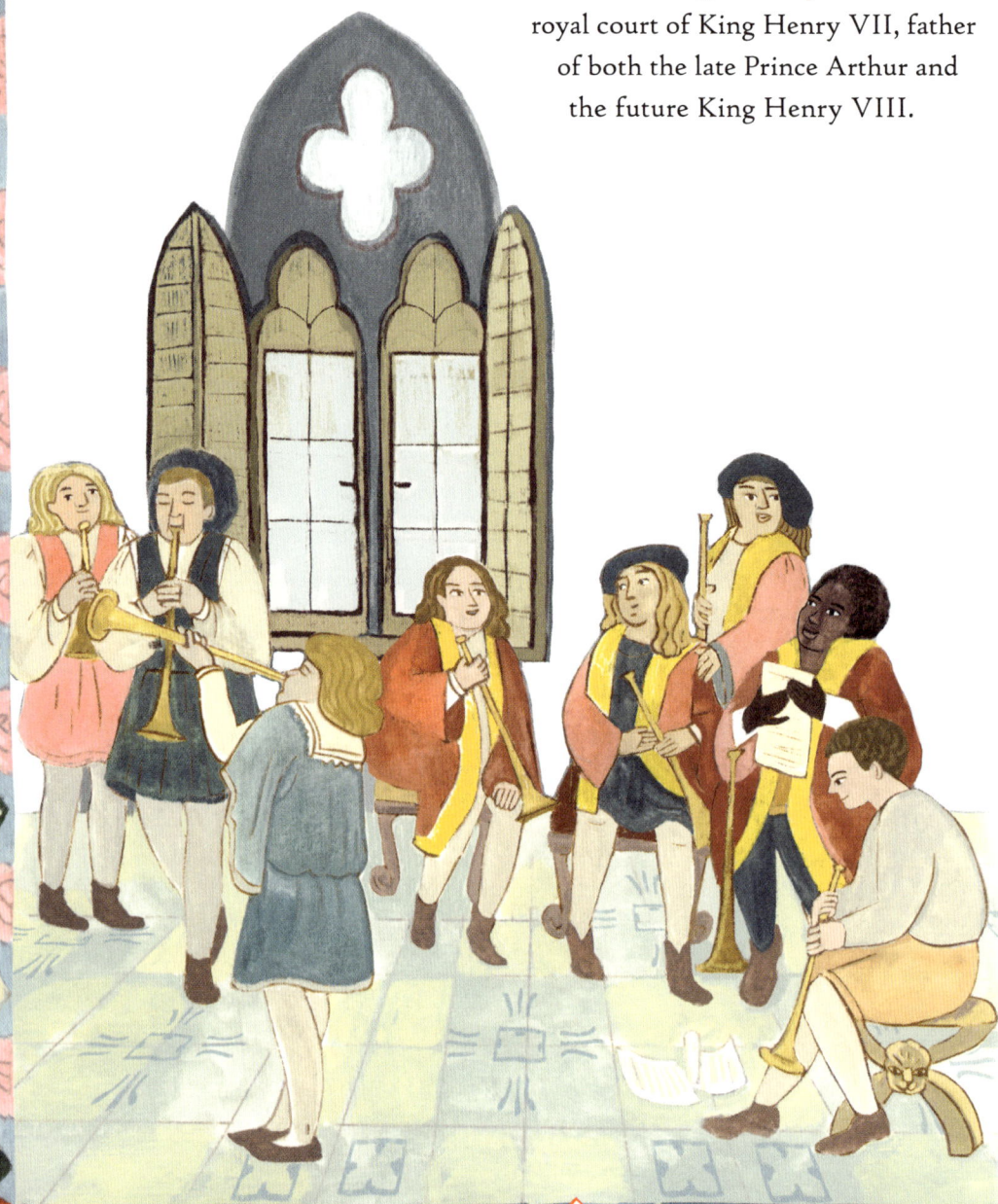

When Henry VII died in April 1509, John played the trumpet at his spectacular funeral ceremony. Finely dressed in black garments bought for the occasion, John and his fellow musicians played their instruments in a grand procession from Richmond to St Paul's Cathedral, and on to Westminster Abbey. The streets thronged with mourners.

Within months, John played in public again, robed in scarlet livery for the joint coronation of King Henry VIII and his new queen: none other than Katherine of Aragon. The wedding feast was a lavish extravaganza. According to a chronicler of the day, as the guests were seated, 'at the bringing of the first course, the trumpets blew up'.

For John, a new reign meant a new opportunity. Aware that his talent and skills had placed him at the very heart of the Tudor court, he seized the chance to ensure that he had his fair reward. He presented a petition to the King, asking for a promotion and a pay rise: 'To the King our sovereign Lord, [i]n most humble wise beseecheth your highness, your true and faithful servant, John Bla[n]ke, one of your trumpets'.

John justified this bold move by reminding the King of his loyalty. He emphasised the 'true and faithful service which your servant daily doeth unto your Grace and so during his life intendeth to do.' Henry was clearly impressed. He signed the agreement as requested, doubling John's pay from 8 pence to 16 pence a day!

On 1 January 1511, it was announced that Queen Katherine had given birth to a baby boy – an heir to the throne. The royal family celebrated by hosting a lavish celebration. The Westminster Tournament was two days of jousting, feasting, pomp and pageantry. John and his fourteen fellow trumpeters, adorned in silver and gold livery, played fanfares for the feasts, the fighting and the festivities.

Thanks to a special record of these celebrations, we know more about John Blanke today. The Westminster Tournament Roll is a long scroll made from thirty-six animal skins. It is richly decorated with painted scenes of the jousting competition organised by Henry VIII to celebrate the birth of his son. At the beginning of the roll, John Blanke appears, astride a horse, playing his trumpet as he heralds the royal couple's arrival. At the end of the roll, John appears again, as his music closes the festivities. Imagine how that royal music might have sounded, accompanied by the clash of jousting lances on armour and frenzied cheers from the crowd!

John Blanke married in Greenwich in January 1512. So valued was he by the court as 'our trumpeter' that the King gave him a personal wedding gift of violet cloth, as well as a hat and a bonnet. We do not know who John's wife was, or what happened to him after that, as his marriage record is the last view we have of his life. It is possible that he may have perished in the fire that destroyed the living quarters at Westminster Palace in 1512. Or perhaps he 'retired' from playing and moved out of public view.

These fragmented written records, together with the extraordinary images on the Westminster Tournament Roll, offer us a unique glimpse into the life of an African man making his mark in Tudor England. That this musician had the courage to present the King himself with a petition for promotion and fair pay reveals that John Blanke knew well the value of his contribution. Whatever John's final years held for him, he has left us with an indelible impression of a royal musician dedicated to his craft; a bright and brilliant star performer.

The Elizabethans to the Georgians

POWERFUL AFRICAN KINGDOMS

In the sixteenth century, while Queen Elizabeth I was building England's influence on the international stage, Africa was home to many powerful kingdoms. Illustrious empires such as Benin and Oyo (in modern-day Nigeria), Akan (Ghana) and Dahomey (Benin) were strong, proud and culturally rich nations. They were also rich in natural resources such as wood, ivory and gold.

THE BEGINNINGS OF TRANSATLANTIC SLAVERY

Meanwhile, explorers from Europe were travelling the globe. As trade routes expanded, European merchants were increasingly drawn to the wealth to be found in Africa.

At the same time, another trade was beginning to take hold, that would tighten its grip over the centuries to come – the trade in enslaved people. In 1607 Britain set up colonies in Jamestown, Virginia, to grow tobacco and cotton, and in 1627 on the Caribbean island of Barbados, to grow sugar on a huge scale. Sugar was a new commodity with mass appeal back home in Britain. The rise in popularity of drinks such as tea and coffee prompted increased demand for the sweet substance made from the sugar cane plant.

From the seventeenth century onwards, thousands of ships carried millions of people from their homes in West Africa to North America and the Caribbean, to work in captivity on plantations. Enslaved people worked in appalling conditions for no pay. Punishments for any attempts to run away, or the slightest 'misdemeanour', were violent and frequent. In 1661 Britain passed a series of laws known as the Barbados Slave

Code, which set out an invented racial hierarchy placing white (Christian) Europeans at the top and enslaved Africans at the bottom. This document introduced the notion of race, of 'whiteness' and 'blackness', in opposition for the first time, creating a framework for structural racism.

THE TRIANGULAR TRADE GROWS

The slave society was soon extended to other islands, such as Jamaica and St Lucia, and a triangular trade was established, prioritising profit over human life. Ships left British port cities such as London, Liverpool, Bristol and Cardiff, equipped with guns, luxury fabrics and glass beads. These were exchanged for men, women and children, who were snatched from their families, chained and crammed onto ships bound for the Americas. Many did not survive the horrific journey through what the Europeans called the 'Middle Passage'. On arrival in the Caribbean and North America, people were sold as property to work on the plantations. The sugar, rum, cotton and tobacco their labour produced was shipped back to Britain.

SETTLEMENT, SERVITUDE AND RESISTANCE

Throughout the eighteenth century, Britain's Black population grew, as African sailors and enslaved people accompanied traders on journeys back to Britain. Some stayed here as enslaved domestic servants; some were free; and some occupied a strange kind of in-between state of servitude due to blurred lines in British law.

But in the Caribbean, in North America, and in Britain, many people rose up and resisted their enslavement in myriad ways: most notably, rebelling, running away, and writing against slavery.

Ignatius Sancho

(1729–1780)

J.S.

LETTER-WRITER, MUSIC-MAKER,
SHOP-KEEPER, VOTER

In 1729, a ship left the emerald-forested coast of West Africa and crossed the Atlantic Ocean. Like thousands of ships before and after, it carried hundreds of African people towards a life of enslaved labour on the sugar plantations of the Caribbean. On that unhappy ship, it is said a baby boy was born.

The ship docked in Cartagena, Colombia. There, the child was baptised Ignatius – 'the fiery one'. Ignatius's parents died soon after, but their flame would live on to burn brightly.

From Cartagena, Ignatius was taken to England and sold to three sisters who lived in Greenwich, London. Many households in eighteenth-century Britain bought and held African people as enslaved servants. Dressed up in extravagant, 'exotic' silks to show off a family's wealth, people were treated (or mistreated) like pets. Some were even made to wear brass collars engraved with the family crest – a cruel jewellery indeed.

The sisters nicknamed the young orphan 'Sancho' after Sancho Panza, a comic character in a famous Spanish book. The name was intended as a spiteful joke, but the boy would claim it as his own and wear it with pride.

Ignatius – as this part of his name suggests – was a bright spark. He longed to be able to read and write. Why should he be denied the power of the written word? Why should he not learn about the world? Education can inspire people to think for themselves. The sisters knew that an educated child might seek his freedom, and so they kept books out of his reach.

But Ignatius's fortunes would turn on a chance meeting. Nearby, in Blackheath, lived the Duke of Montagu with his family. A wealthy man, he possessed an extraordinary personal library. When they met, Ignatius made such an impression on the Duke that he invited Ignatius to visit his library and borrow his books. Ignatius – curious, and quick to learn – lost himself in literature. It was to be a lifelong love.

'Improve
your mind
with good
reading'

As Ignatius approached the age of twenty, the Duke died. Desperate to leave the cruel sisters, Ignatius begged the Duchess for help. After relentless persuasion, she hired him as her butler. Ignatius thrived at the centre of a bustling household. He cultivated a lively network of friends: musicians, artists, writers; working and well-to-do; Black and white.

Ignatius became valet to the new Duke of Montagu – the first Duke's son-in-law – and earned enough money to live independently. Dazzled by a passion for the theatre, he apparently once spent his last shilling on a ticket to see his friend, the famous actor David Garrick, play Shakespeare's Richard III at the Theatre Royal, Drury Lane.

On a visit to the grand, golden-stoned city of Bath, Ignatius had his portrait painted by the celebrated artist Thomas Gainsborough. Rare for its time, this powerful painting places Ignatius centre stage in a dignified depiction of a Black man.

'I am not ashamed to own that I love my wife'

Ignatius Sancho bought a grocery store in the heart of Westminster. Owning property gave him the right to vote. He voted in 1774, and again in 1780. He may have been the first Black person to vote in a British parliamentary election!

Ignatius and his wife – Ann Osborne, a free Caribbean woman – raised a large loving family. Theirs was a harmonious household: the children – the 'Sanchonets and Sanchonettas' – were often seen helping out in the shop or playing music on the family harpsichord.

Music flourished in the eighteenth century. Concert halls rang with the operas and oratorios of Handel; Mozart's minuets swept through the ballrooms of the land. We know from newspapers of the time that Black people came together for spectacular dances in local taverns and London parks. Ignatius was a keen composer of classical music. He wrote sweet-toned songs and delicate dance tunes for performance at parties and public events. He even noted dance steps onto the pages of his music!

The eighteenth century came to be known
as a golden age of letter-writing. Letters written
by famous people were published in books for everyone
to read. Ignatius penned endless letters to his many friends.
Written 'to the ringing of the shop-bell', they sparkled and fizzed with
tales of London life in all its grime and glory. The streets surrounding
the Sanchos' shop thronged with sights and sounds. Carriages clattered
over cobbles, and the cries of street sellers coloured the air from dawn till
dusk. Ignatius was a witty witness to daily events, ranging from royal
ceremonies to political riots. Playful puns prowled through his paragraphs
– dashes dictated dramatic pauses – exclamations abounded!

Ignatius was fiercely proud of his African identity, signing his letters to newspapers: 'Africanus'. As a wise elder, he advised and encouraged fellow Africans living in the city. As a literary critic, he praised poetry. He described the brutal treatment of African people on West Indian plantations, calling the 'wicked' trade in enslaved people 'a subject that sours my blood'. He wrote to the famous novelist Laurence Sterne, asking him to write about the evils of slavery. Sterne did so, and when Sterne's letters were published, Ignatius's name shot to prominence.

Life for a Black family in Georgian London still had its challenges. Of a family outing to the fashionable Vauxhall Pleasure Gardens, Ignatius mused that they 'were gazed at, followed etc etc but not much abused'.

He wrote tenderly of Ann and of the children. But not all the Sancho children survived to see adulthood. Kitty died at the age of just five after months of illness. Though grief and poverty were never far from the door, Ignatius and Ann stayed strong, and held on to happiness. Of their new baby son Billy, Ignatius wrote fondly: 'he is like his father – fat – heavy – sleepy'. Did Ignatius ever dream that his son, William Leach Osborne, would grow up to become the first Black publisher in the Western world?

As he grew older, Ignatius became ill with gout – a painful swelling disease – yet he faced even his own death with characteristic courage. Ignatius's letters were published soon after his death. His writing would become a powerful tool for the Abolitionist movement to demonstrate the outstanding intellectual capabilities of African people. Today, we still value Ignatius Sancho's vibrant voice.

'I am Sir an Affrican – with two ffs – if you please – and proud am I'

Olaudah Equiano
(1745–1797)

SAILOR · AUTOBIOGRAPHER · ABOLITIONIST

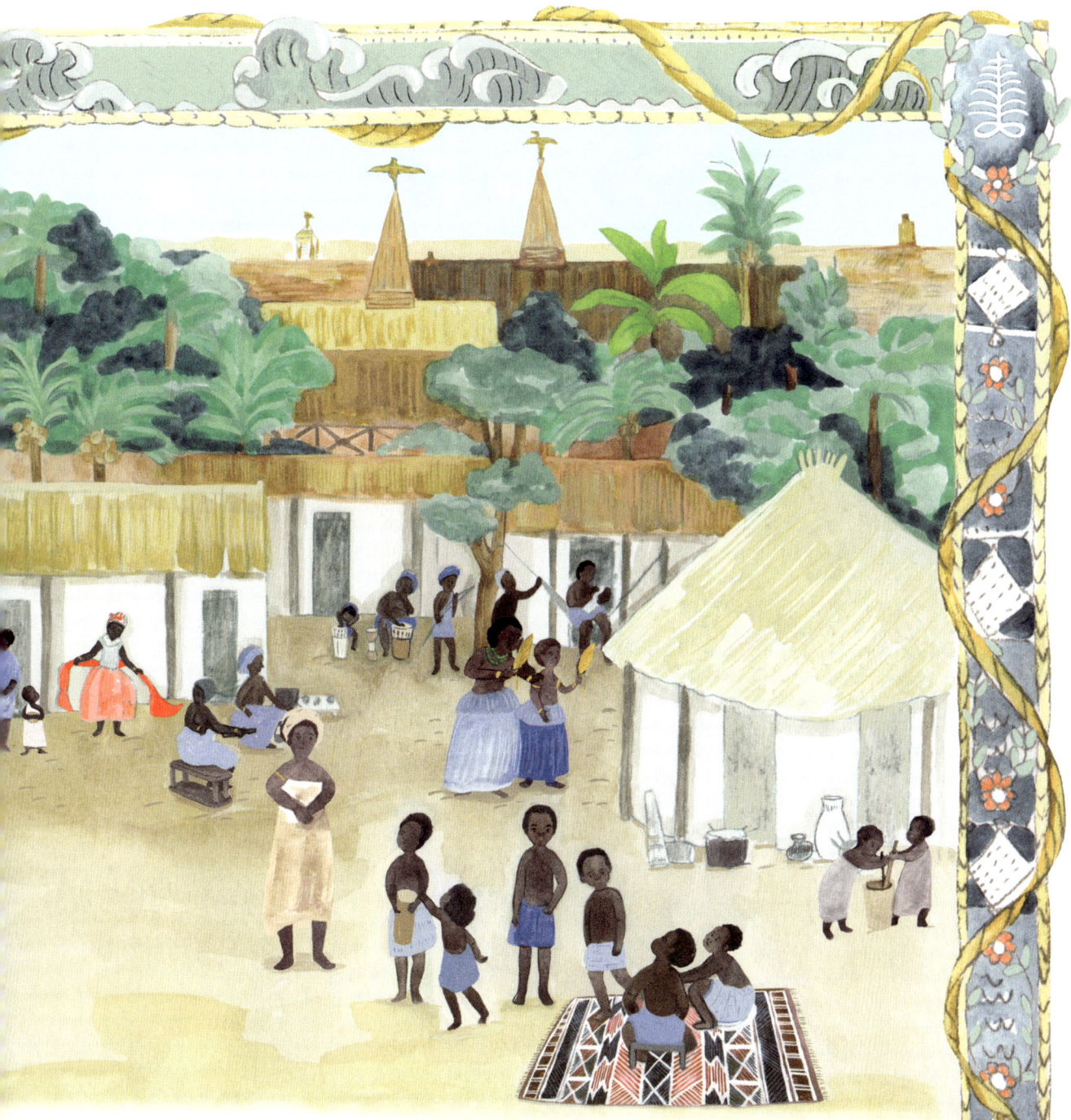

According to his action-packed autobiography, *The Interesting Narrative of the Life of Olaudah Equiano*, Olaudah was born in the kingdom of Benin – a 'nation of dancers, musicians and poets'. The youngest son of seven children in a learned Igbo family, he enjoyed a harmonious childhood in a prosperous society, where busy cities thrived in fertile, fruitful land.

But his peaceful life of pleasure and play was shattered when he and his only sister were snatched from their home in a slave raid. After a terrifying ordeal in the dark, dank hold of a slave-ship bound for the Caribbean, brother and sister were separated and sold into enslavement in Barbados.

Olaudah tells of being taken to Virginia, then a British colony in America, where the tobacco industry drove the terrible trade in people. There he was 'bought' by a Royal Navy captain who treated Olaudah more like property than a person. He renamed him Gustavus Vassa, after a Swedish king – a cruel joke of a name. Olaudah resisted. The captain responded with violence. For now, the name would stick. But this strong-willed young man held tight to his right to be free.

In the years that followed, Olaudah sailed the seas of the world from north to south, from east to west. He witnessed island uprisings and fought in naval battles.

'I had often seen my master and [my friend] Dick employed in reading; and I had a great curiosity to talk to the books, as I thought they did'

But it was also on board a ship that he determined to learn to read. He had seen others around him 'employed in reading'. What was this magic power that books seemed to have over people? Olaudah knew that learning to read and write the language of those now around him held the key to his freedom. Surely, once he arrived in London, he could go free? When the ship docked in Deptford, his heart was full of hope.

But the captain had other plans. He had already cut a deal and sold Olaudah to another man. Olaudah was forced onto a ship bound for the Caribbean island of Montserrat. Disappointed, disillusioned, and devastated by the treatment of Africans he witnessed, Olaudah made himself a promise: he would do everything he could to obtain his freedom and return to England.

Sold from one captain to another, he worked as a valet, a sailor and a soldier. His travels around the Americas took him to Philadelphia, Georgia, New Providence, Martinique, Grenada and Jamaica.

In the face of each fresh challenge, Olaudah invented himself anew. Everywhere he went, he formed bonds of friendship. Determined to survive – and to thrive – he took his fate into his own hands. Observing the business deals of sailors and merchants, Olaudah learned how to buy and sell goods to make his own money, saving scrupulously to 'purchase' his freedom.

'I determined to make every exertion to obtain my freedom, and to return to Old England'

In Montserrat in 1766, Olaudah paid £40 – nearly £6,000 in today's money – for a 'letter of manumission' granting him his liberty. Free at last! Olaudah hosted a dance party to celebrate the exciting event, noting in his narrative how impressive he looked in his 'Georgia superfine blue clothes'.

Now a free man, he could earn his own money as a highly skilled sailor. His love of the ocean led him on voyages to Portugal, Spain, Turkey, and even the Arctic! But danger and deception lurked around every corner. After navigating for many years the choppy waters of a life as an African man among mercenary merchants and treacherous traders, Olaudah set his sights on returning to England for good.

'I was named Olaudah, which in
our language signifies ... fortunate,
also one favoured and having
a loud voice and well spoken'

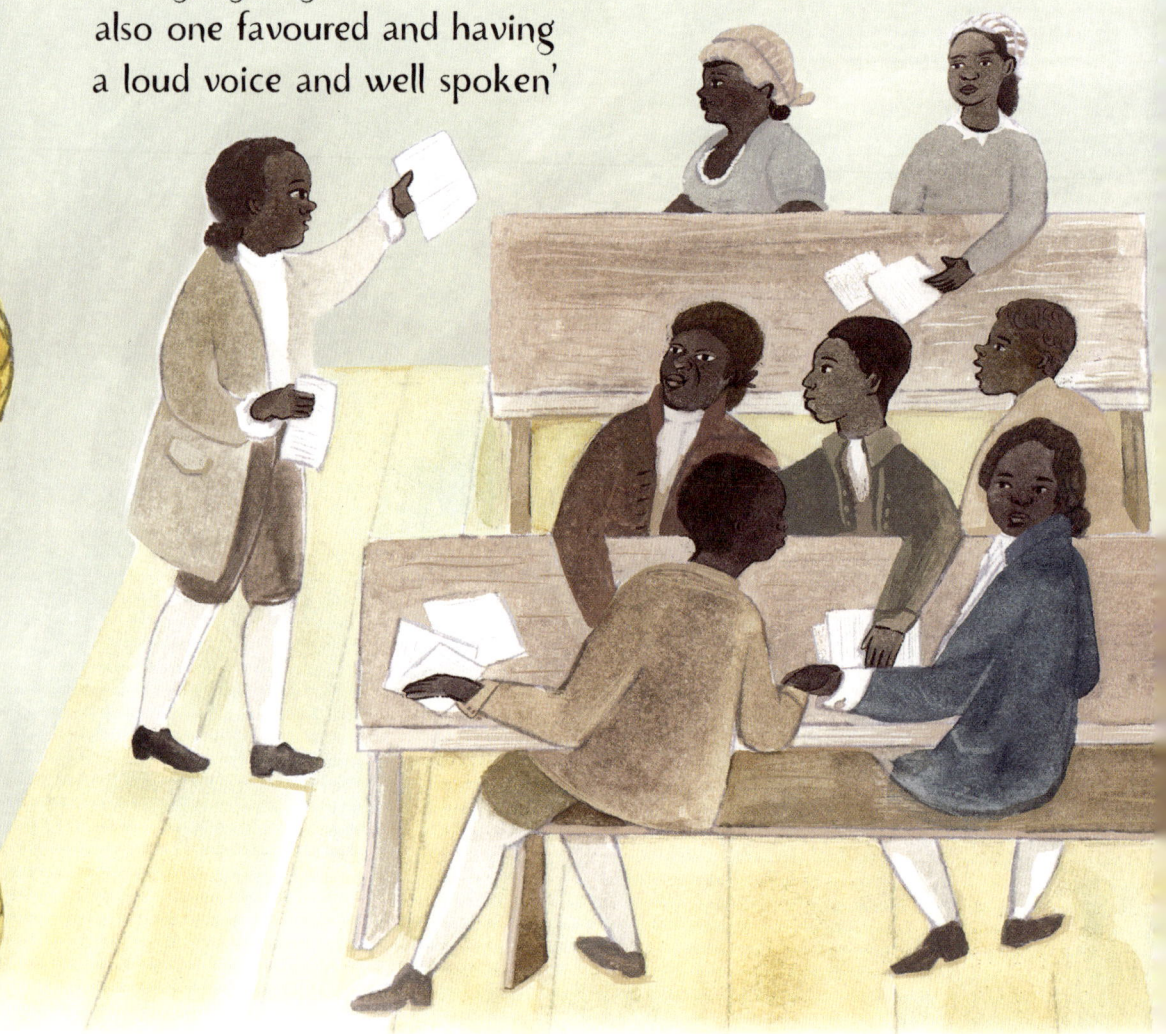

Arriving in London in 1777, he joined a Black population of around
twenty thousand people: some were free, but others were still enslaved.
Olaudah rallied comrades round him to form a political movement
called the 'Sons of Africa'. These African activists worked tirelessly
towards the abolition of slavery. They gave detailed testimony of their
personal experiences of enslavement, and demanded its end. In 1787,

Ottobah Cugoano, another famous Son of Africa, published a scathing condemnation of slavery, *Thoughts and Sentiments on the Evil and Wicked Traffic of the Slavery and Commerce of the Human Species*. Together, he and Olaudah wrote letters to royals, politicians and influential people of the day. They lobbied Parliament, and Olaudah even presented a petition to Queen Charlotte, wife of King George III, who herself had African ancestry.

In 1783, Olaudah exposed the tragic scandal of the *Zong*, a slaving ship, from which over one hundred and thirty living African men, women and children had been thrown overboard to their deaths by the captain and crew in an insurance scam.

In addition, when the British government designed a scheme to send freed Africans from London to Freetown, Sierra Leone, Olaudah made public the corruption behind the operation.

As the debate in Parliament on slavery grew more fierce and more divided, Olaudah sought new ways to raise up that 'loud' and 'well spoken' voice for social justice. And so, in 1789, this remarkable man, who called himself 'neither a saint, nor a hero, nor a tyrant', published his autobiography. His portrait was engraved on the front page, and his real name was confirmed in print for posterity.

Olaudah knew that to persuade people to buy the book, he had to publicise it. He travelled throughout Britain and Ireland, captivating audiences with his compelling life story. Word spread like wildfire. People flocked to hear what this elegant, eloquent man, who had survived so many struggles and witnessed so many wonders, had to say. He practically invented the book tour! And his powers of persuasion were mighty. The 'Interesting Narrative' sold out nine editions in his lifetime alone, and rapidly became a crucial weapon in the fight to abolish slavery.

In 1792, Olaudah Equiano married Susanna Cullen, an Englishwoman from Soham, a small village in Cambridgeshire. They settled in Soham and had two daughters, but both Susanna and elder daughter Anna died in 1796. After an extraordinary life of adventure and the overcoming of many obstacles, Olaudah followed them to his rest the following year. His daughter Joanna, however, though orphaned at the age of two, lived long to enjoy the freedom that her fearless father had worked so hard to achieve.

Dido Elizabeth Belle

(1761–1804)

AN HEIRESS OF MIXED HERITAGE IN HAMPSTEAD

Imagine living in a mansion complete with its own woods, ponds, stables, a dairy, and even a library! Such was the life of Dido Elizabeth Belle, a young lady growing up in Georgian London.

Dido was born to an African mother and a white British father in 1761, when Britain's involvement in the slave trade was at its height. Dido's mother, Maria Belle (or Bell), had been enslaved in the Caribbean when she met Sir John Lindsay, an officer in the Royal Navy.

One account from a family acquaintance relates
that Maria and John arrived in London together before
Dido was born. At the age of five, Dido was baptised at
John's family church, St George's, in the central London
district of Bloomsbury. Perhaps because her parents were
not married, Dido was taken into the care of John's aunt
and uncle, Lady Elizabeth Murray and Lord William
Murray, Earl of Mansfield. The Mansfields split their
time between their home in Bloomsbury and their
Hampstead Heath mansion, Kenwood House,
an oasis of calm overlooking the bustling city.

What did life hold for this young girl,
born into such extraordinary circumstances?

Her cousin, Elizabeth Mary, had also joined the Mansfield household, after her mother died young. With no children of their own, the Mansfields welcomed their two young protégées with warmth. The girls were close companions, but – as a young Black woman living in eighteenth-century Britain, and the daughter of unmarried parents – Dido's social position was more precarious.

Did young Dido ever see her mother or her father again? We cannot be sure. Maria may have remained in London and spent time with Dido. However, by the time Dido was a teenager, her mother had purchased her own freedom and was living in Pensacola, Florida, on land bought by John Lindsay.

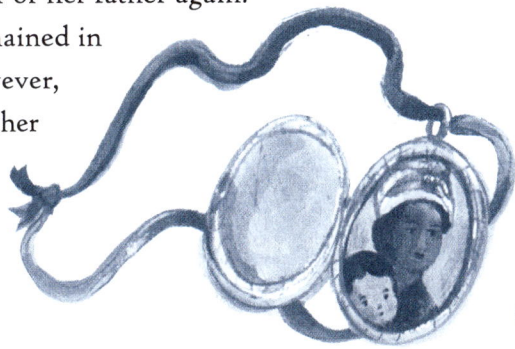

Kenwood House, surrounded by lush green gardens, shimmering ponds and verdant woods, was a majestic mansion built to look like a classical temple. Dido was raised there as a 'gentlewoman': educated by private tutors to develop 'accomplishments' such as reading and reciting poetry, speaking French, playing the piano, and horse-riding. She also looked after the dairy, where cream and butter were made from the milk of the family's small herd of longhorn cows!

Kenwood boasted a magnificent library. Dido could take her pick of hundreds of books, at a time when very few people could read or write. And how she loved reading! A guest at the house once commented on Dido's brilliant after-dinner poetry performance at the age of just ten.

And Dido's handwriting was so elegant that her great-uncle would ask her to scribe his letters for him!

47

It was often noted that Lord Mansfield had a deep affection for his great-niece. And this family tie gave Dido a unique view of a most pressing political issue. Lord Mansfield was the Lord Chief Justice – the most powerful judge in England. He presided over several cases that sparked fiery debates about slavery and freedom.

James Somerset – an African man who had escaped enslavement – was recaptured in London in 1771 by his former 'master' Charles Stewart and imprisoned on a boat bound for the sugar plantations of Jamaica. Somerset challenged Stewart's right to force him back into slavery. The abolitionist Granville Sharp helped Somerset in court, and the case captured public attention on a grand scale. As presiding judge, Lord Mansfield had to decide who should win the case.

Which way would Mansfield rule? After much deliberation, he ruled in favour of James Somerset, making it illegal to force a free or freed person in Britain into enslavement in the Caribbean. Black people celebrated the decision with parties in taverns around the city.

As the only family member of colour living in her household, Dido must have felt the decision keenly. When Lord Mansfield died in 1793, he confirmed Dido's freedom in his will. He left her £500, but granted £10,000 to her cousin Elizabeth, revealing just how precarious Dido's status was, both in society and within her own family.

Later that year, Dido married a French servant, named Jean Louis Davinier. The couple set up home in the central London district of Pimlico. Her new life was a far cry from the grandeur and opulence of the aristocratic household at Kenwood, but Dido made a family home for herself, becoming a mother and raising her sons, Charles (whose twin, John, sadly died in infancy) and young William Thomas.

Dido died in 1804 at the age of just forty-three. Sadly, no obituary for her exists, but her father's obituary reveals the uplifting effect she had on those who met her: '[her] amiable disposition and accomplishments have gained her the highest respect from all his Lordship's relations and visitants'.

Perhaps Dido's most compelling legacy is the intriguing portrait painted by Scottish artist David Martin of the two girl cousins. Elizabeth sits, a book open on her lap, staring straight at the viewer. Dido, dressed in 'exotic' costume, holds a bowl of fruit and flowers – at first glance, a stereotypical depiction of Black people of the time. However, Dido is not painted at the edge or the bottom of the canvas. Instead, she rushes out of the picture, her scarf billowing freely behind her. The pose is energetic, playful, surprising. She holds our gaze with an enigmatic smile, her finger pointing to the smooth brown skin of her cheek. Her dark eyes sparkle with mischief and fun.

Dido compels us to look at her, challenging our assumptions about who she was, as she gestures to the conundrum of her identity. Born to an enslaved mother and an aristocratic father, raised as a gentlewoman in an immensely powerful household, and dying in obscurity before her legacy was revived, Dido Belle embodied the complexities and contradictions of being Black and British in the eighteenth century.

Mary Prince
(1788–after 1833)

A STORYTELLING FREEDOM FIGHTER

Mary Prince was born into an African family, enslaved in Brackish Pond, Bermuda, in around 1788. Her father worked at a nearby shipbuilding yard, while she lived with her mother and siblings in the household of a sea captain. Mary was given as a 'gift' to the captain's granddaughter, a little girl her own age, who treated her like a pet.

Knowing no other life, Mary did not immediately grasp the gravity of her situation: 'I was too young to understand rightly my condition as a slave, and too thoughtless and full of spirits to look forward to the days of toil and sorrow'. Indeed, the captain had a harsh nature; everyone in the household feared his returns from sea. When his wife died, he sold Mary and her siblings at auction to raise money for a wedding to a new wife. Mary later wrote of the pain of being separated from her family: 'I cannot bear to think of that day... It recalls the great grief that filled my heart ... whilst listening to the pitiful words of my poor mother, weeping for the loss of her children'.

The next family was even more brutal than the last. After suffering violent beatings, and witnessing many more, Mary decided enough was enough. One night she crept out of the house and fled back to her mother. It was a courageous move in extremely dangerous circumstances: fugitivity was often met with severe punishment. Mary's mother hid her away in a rocky cave, bringing her food at night in secret, but when Mary's father heard that she was hiding as a fugitive, he took her back to her tormentors. He begged them to forgive her: his words fell on deaf ears. Five more years of cruel treatment followed.

Mary was sold on again to a man at Grand Turk Island, some 900 miles from Bermuda. There, she was set to work in the salt ponds. Salt was in great demand, to preserve food and prevent it from rotting in the heat. The work was arduous. People stood all day in the ponds under the blazing sun: the salt ate into their skin. As Mary recalled, 'Our feet and legs, from standing in the salt water for so many hours, soon became full of dreadful boils'.

One day a boat arrived at the island, bringing more people to work in the salt ponds: Mary's mother was among them. But the reunion Mary hoped for was not to be. Her mother's mind was so shattered by the ordeals of her life and the loss of her children that when she saw Mary, she did not recognise her own daughter.

'All slaves want to be free –
to be free is very sweet'

Some years later, Mary travelled to the island of
Antigua with the Wood family, the last in a long line
of people to claim her as property. In their house, amid
the insults and violence, she balanced looking after
the children with a heavy load of manual tasks, such as
cooking, cleaning and washing. But her years in the salt
ponds had taken their toll on her flesh. Mary's body
was ravaged by rheumatism. Her joints were screwed
painfully tight, her limbs swollen and disfigured.

An elderly African woman, a neighbour,
came to her aid. Using her specialist knowledge
of medicinal plants, she boiled herbs to heal
Mary's wounds and soothe her suffering.
Mary cherished this woman's care in
her hour of need: 'I don't know what
I should have done, or what would
have become of me, had it not
been for her'.

Seeking spiritual solace in scripture and worship, Mary joined the Moravian Church.

It was at church that Mary met Daniel James, a free Black man, who was a carpenter. The pair fell in love and were married in the Moravian Chapel at Spring Gardens in 1826.

The Woods were enraged that Mary had dared to marry without their permission, and they punished her severely. But Mary staunchly defended her decision. Could she not buy her freedom from them? The Woods refused.

When the Woods decided to send their son to school in England, Mary saw her chance. She crossed the ocean with the family, believing that once she set foot on English soil, she would be free. Then she could sail back to Antigua a free woman to live with her husband. But the Woods would not let her go, insisting that a return to Antigua meant a return to slavery.

Mary was distraught but determined.
Knowing she had nowhere else to live and
no means to support herself, she gathered her
belongings and walked out into the street, away
from the Wood household, head held high. She asked
the Moravian Church in Hatton Garden for help, and
sought sanctuary with the Anti-Slavery Society. There,
she met Thomas Pringle, a journalist, who offered her
work in his house as a domestic servant. Now Mary had
somewhere safe to stay and a means of earning her living.

Mary made two definitive steps towards her own freedom and the freedom of others. Firstly, she petitioned Parliament to allow her to return to the Caribbean a free woman. In fact, she was the first woman to present a petition to Parliament. Women's voices were routinely ignored or silenced by men in power. Women could raise petitions for a cause, but could not sign them. Women could attend public meetings, but if they spoke up, their words were not recorded in writing. Mary's petition was refused, but she gave testimony in court, making sure her side of the story was heard and recorded for posterity.

Then, with the help of Thomas Pringle, Mary published a detailed account of her experiences. Dictated to a woman called Susannah Strickland, who wrote it down for her, Mary's story laid bare the brutality of slavery and spotlighted its impact on the minds and bodies of women and children as well as men. Published in 1831, Mary's powerfully emotive book, *The History of Mary Prince, a West Indian Slave, related by Herself*, was read by thousands – the first full-length narrative published in Britain by a Black woman.

In 1833, Britain would finally pass the Act to abolish slavery in the British colonies. Mary's name did not appear again in written records so we cannot say for certain what she did next. Perhaps she chose to stay in London? Or maybe she returned to Antigua to join her husband? Mary Prince is now a national hero of Bermuda, her legacy lasting well beyond her lifetime.

The Victorians

THE FIGHT FOR FREEDOM

Throughout the eighteenth and nineteenth centuries, African people enslaved in the British Caribbean repeatedly rose up against their oppressors. Revolts such as Tacky's War (Jamaica, 1760–61), Bussa's Rebellion (Barbados, 1816), and the Baptist Wars or Christmas Rebellions (Jamaica, 1831–32) all helped to destabilise the slave system. In Britain, powerful political writing by authors Black and white, animated by rousing speeches, fuelled a huge public anti-slavery campaign.

The Act for the Abolition of the Slave Trade was passed in Parliament in 1807. But, although trading in people was now outlawed, slavery itself continued. In 1833, the Slavery Abolition Act was passed to end the practice of slavery. However, it was followed by a period of enforced 'apprenticeship', which required people to work for a further four to six years without pay. On 1 August 1838, enslaved people across the British Caribbean finally became free.

THE EXPANSION OF EMPIRE

When Queen Victoria came to the throne in 1837, she prioritised the expansion of the British Empire. Britain sought out new trading opportunities across the globe, and, with them, new lands to occupy.

Meanwhile, as the industrialisation of Britain progressed rapidly, the reality remained that much of Britain's wealth still relied heavily on enslaved labour: cotton, a staple of Britain's economy, was grown by enslaved Africans in America, where slavery continued until 1865. That same year, labourers in Morant Bay, Jamaica, launched a rebellion to protest their profound poverty and poor working conditions – the extreme inequities on the island left as a legacy of slavery.

THE SCRAMBLE FOR AFRICA

As the nineteenth century drew to a close, Britain extended its control in Africa through colonisation. In 1884, leaders from Europe, America and the Ottoman Empire met at a conference in Berlin and carved up the continent of Africa between them. By 1900, only a tenth of the land in Africa was ruled by Africans. The rich mix of African languages, cultures and societal structures would be marginalised in favour of British systems of law, education, religion and ways of living. Forty-five million Africans – one third of all Africans – were now British colonial subjects.

Mary Seacole

(1805–1881)

WARTIME NURSE AND WORLD TRAVELLER

Mary Seacole was baptised Mary Jane Grant in 1805 in
Kingston, Jamaica. Her mother, Rebecca, was a Jamaican
doctress – a woman skilled in using herbs for healing.
Mary's father, John, was a Scottish army officer. As Jamaica was still a
British colony, many British soldiers and sailors were stationed on the
island. Mary and her mother were members of a free Creole population.

Rebecca was one of many Jamaican women with exceptional
knowledge of the herbs, fruits and barks of the island. She used her
special skills in combining and preparing them to bring out their powerful
properties. As a small child, Mary was captivated by her mother's work:
'I was very young when I began to make use of the little knowledge I had
acquired from watching my mother, upon a great sufferer – my doll,' she
wrote. 'Before long it was very natural that I should seek to extend my
practice; and so I found other patients in the dogs and cats around me'.

'I have never been long in any place before
I have found my practical experience
in the science of medicine useful'

Rebecca ran a boarding-house in Kingston where soldiers came
for care and convalescence when ill or injured. As she grew older, Mary
assisted her mother in tending soldiers and their families. Rebecca's
healing wisdom and nursing skills passed from mother to daughter as
Mary learned to mix medicines, prepare poultices and tend wounds.

Mary's desire for travel began young. She travelled from Kingston to London twice, taking Caribbean pickles and preserves to sell in England, revealing an early entrepreneurial spirit. She also visited the Bahamas, Haiti and Cuba, where she bought goods that she would take home to sell.

Back in Jamaica, Mary married Edwin Horatio Seacole, who was a godson of Lord Admiral Horatio Nelson. But Edwin fell very ill. In spite of intense care from Mary and other medical practitioners, he died. Mary was greatly grieved. When her mother died soon after, Mary felt alone in the world, but resolved to follow the path that lay ahead.

When cholera, a highly contagious and deadly disease, ripped through Jamaica in 1850, Mary witnessed at close hand its devastating effects, and made mental notes. Meanwhile, her brother Edward had moved to Cruces, Panama, to set up a store and boarding-house. Many people looking for gold in California passed through Panama, and Mary saw an opportunity to run her own business. Armed with provisions made in her kitchen to sell – pickles and preserves, medicines and herbal remedies – she made the difficult journey to join her brother.

But diseases travel fast and cholera soon landed in Cruces. As people began to fall sick and die, Mary stepped into her calling. She developed effective remedies using mustard powder, calomel and cinnamon water to heal her patients. She promoted healthy eating and established methods of hygiene, such as opening windows to air rooms where the disease had taken hold. Here, as she was to write later in her travelogue, she saved her first life.

Such was the need for Mary's skills that she bought a property and set up her own 'hotel', where she sold remedies and could tend to the sick. Now Mary was securing a reputation as a skilled doctress developing highly effective methods to combat infection and disease.

She returned to Jamaica, where she treated patients during an outbreak of yellow fever at Up Park Camp, the British Army headquarters. Her boarding-house became a busy hospital, and Mary built friendships with many of her patients, dedicating her life to her nursing practice.

In 1853, war broke out in the Crimea between Russia and Turkey. France, Sardinia and Britain sent troops to the Crimea to help Turkey defend itself from Russian invasion. British soldiers who were stationed in Jamaica prepared to leave. Mary felt compelled to join the soldiers, who had come to know her as 'Mother Seacole'.

Mary travelled to London and presented herself to the War Office, with letters of recommendation acknowledging her outstanding devotion and exceptional skill. Her application was ignored. She heard that a nurse called Florence Nightingale had travelled to the Crimea, and applied to join her ranks of nurses. She was refused. After a fruitless interview with one of Nightingale's representatives, she wrote: 'I read in her face the fact that, had there been a vacancy, I should not have been chosen to fill it'.

BRITISH HOTEL

Mrs. Mary Seacole
(Late of Kingston, Jamaica),
Respectfully announces to her former kind friends, and to the Officers of the Army and Navy generally, That she has taken her passage in the screw-steamer 'Hollander', to start from London on the 25th of January, intending on her arrival at Balaclava to establish a mess table and comfortable quarters for sick and convalescent officers.

Undeterred, Mary decided to fund the trip herself. Using her own money and resources, she set up a hospital near Balaclava, running a large-scale operation close to the front lines. Brightly dressed in yellow, blue and red, so that she could easily be spotted, she nursed soldiers on the battlefields. She even risked her life under fire to treat fighters where they fell. In her travelogue, she recorded her first-hand account of the Crimean war and its horrors.

'I shall make no excuse to my readers for giving
them a pretty full history of my struggles
to become a Crimean heroine'

After the war, Mary returned to London, her funds depleted by her operation in the Crimea. A grand gala was held in 1857 to raise money to repay her. The event took place over four days on the banks of the River Thames and was attended by over eighty thousand people, with an estimated one thousand performers entertaining the crowds. However, the event was so extravagant that Mary only received a small sum of money from its profits.

That same year, Mary published her travelogue, *Wonderful Adventures of Mrs Seacole in Many Lands*. By writing her own memoirs, she recorded an extraordinary account of an adventurous life's work of courage, commitment, and care for others.

In later years, Mary was favoured by the royal family, and became personal masseuse to Princess Alexandra. In 1881, Mary died at her home in Paddington. She had been an outstanding pioneer in the medical profession, building on her knowledge of Caribbean medicine to develop clinical techniques that are valued globally today. She is still a powerful role model for nurses and doctors, from Jamaica to Britain and beyond, and was honoured in 2016 with a statue at St Thomas' Hospital in London.

Ira Aldridge

(1807–1867)

AFRICAN AMERICAN ACTOR

AND ACTIVIST

Ira Aldridge was born in 1807 in New York, to free African American parents, Daniel and Luranah. Daniel was a preacher at Old Zion, the city's African Church.

When Ira was ten, his mother died and his father remarried. Grief-stricken, Ira ran away from home, sailing alone from New York to North Carolina, a state where slavery was still legal. There, a slave-dealer tried to buy him for $500. The ship's captain came to the boy's rescue, insisting that he had promised to take Ira back to New York. A lucky escape from a very different life...

Back in New York and reunited with his father, Ira attended the African Free School, which was founded for African American children by the New York Manumission Society. Ira's eloquence and dramatic skills won him a prize at school for 'declamation' – excellent public speaking – and he was encouraged by his teacher to pursue a theatrical career.

Ira soon discovered the theatres of New York. Most theatres in the USA denied access to Black people, but at the Chatham, Ira was allowed to watch from the wings and help the actors with their costumes, while at the Park Theatre he gazed down from the balcony, spellbound by performances of Shakespeare's plays. What extraordinary opportunities for a young boy to see the magic of theatrical life up close!

In 1821, Ira joined the African Grove Theatre Company, a new troupe established by James Hewlett and members of a growing free Black community in New York. This was a Black-led theatre company, where actors and audience members alike could participate freely. Ira was transfixed by Hewlett's performances of Othello and Richard III. The young actor had found the inspiration he sought: Black actors performing centre stage in classical roles. But the local sheriff launched a sustained campaign of racial harassment and hostility. After repeated arrests without cause, and a number of violent assaults on its members, the Grove Theatre was closed.

It was clear to Ira that his opportunities to shine on the American stage were limited and fraught with potential trouble. In 1824, he took work as a steward on a ship to Liverpool, England. From there, full of ambition, he travelled to London to launch his acting career. At the age of seventeen, Ira made his debut on the London stage in the role of Othello at the Royalty Theatre in the East End. This moment marked the first recorded instance of a Black man taking a lead Shakespearean role on stage in Britain.

From there, Ira moved swiftly on to the Royal Coburg Theatre – later known as The Old Vic – to play Oroonoko, the character of an African prince, in an adaptation of an anti-slavery play by female playwright Aphra Behn.

That same year, he met and married Margaret Gill, an Englishwoman from Northallerton, Yorkshire, described by a friend as 'an intelligent lady of fine accomplishments and great conversational talent'.

'He desires only to be judged by his actions, and relies on that discrimination and generosity which appreciates endeavour and rewards effort'

When Ira reprised the role of Othello, this time at the Theatre Royal in Brighton, a local newspaper review hailed him as 'an actor of real and undoubted talent... [A]lthough his voice was loud and energetic, his style was perfectly free from extravagance'. Ira was beginning to develop his own unique style of acting, far from the exaggerated styles that had previously been popular. His new acting style was full of feeling, yet naturalistic; his sonorous voice emitted emotion; his compelling characterisation connected deeply with audiences. Ira's fresh interpretations of iconic tragic roles paved the way for future actors.

The character of Othello, an African general in the Venetian army, had traditionally been played by white men in blackface make-up. Physical performances were often exaggerated and they heavily reinforced negative stereotypes of Black men. Ira, however, delivered a more subtle and sympathetic performance, portraying Othello as a complex human being. He also adapted playscripts in order to expand and improve the representation of his characters. Inspired by his early admiration for James Hewlett, he played roles such as King Lear and Macbeth, which had for many years been considered the preserve of white actors.

While public debate raged between pro-slavery lobbyists and abolitionists, Ira's powerful performances were becoming a force to be reckoned with. As Ira became increasingly popular with theatre-goers, the press began to take against him, peppering their newspaper reviews with racist insults. The effect was devastating. Soon, even London theatres were closing their doors against him.

Undeterred, Ira toured his work – still popular with audiences –
all around Britain and Ireland. In 1827, he performed in Manchester,
Lancaster, Sheffield and Newcastle. In later years he led a theatre troupe
to Dublin and on a tour of Scotland. At the end of each performance,
Ira would give a farewell speech, condemning the injustice of slavery
and sharing with the audience his hopes for a future without prejudice.
And Ira was a man of action as well as words. A passionate advocate
for freedom, he sent money regularly to the United States to buy
manumission documents for enslaved families.

Ira's fame and popularity continued to grow. In 1852, he left England with his wife and son to tour Europe, packing out theatres in Sweden, Germany, Poland – where he was especially revered – and Russia. He invited actors to speak their lines in their own languages for the benefit of the audience. In Poland, he was affectionately named 'brother', perhaps for his sympathy with Polish resistance to Russian rule.

Ira was granted British citizenship in 1863. After the death of his wife Margaret, he remarried, to a concert singer named Amanda Brandt. He continued to tour, but on a visit to Poland in 1867 he fell ill with a lung infection, and died on 7 August, aged sixty. The *Warsaw Courier* reported that he passed away 'peacefully and painlessly'. Such was Ira's legacy in Poland that he was given a state funeral; on its eve, the Polish Society of Singers sang him to his rest. Ira was survived by four children. Among them was Amanda Aldridge, a concert singer who would go on to teach elocution to the legendary African American actor Paul Robeson – an apt epilogue to Ira's thrilling theatrical legacy.

Omoba Aina
(Sarah Forbes Bonetta)

(1843–1880)

AN AFRICAN PRINCESS
AND 'PERFECT GENIUS'

Sarah Forbes Bonetta was born Omoba Aina, in around 1843, to a royal family from the Egbado clan of the Yoruba people in Nigeria. When King Ghezo of Dahomey, a large West African kingdom in present-day Benin, launched a slave raid on her village, Aina's family were killed and she was taken captive.

Ten years earlier, in 1833, a law had been passed to abolish slavery in the British colonies. Now Britain was keen to present itself as a noble nation dedicated to stopping the trade in enslaved people, while continuing to expand the British Empire through colonial conquest. The West Africa squadron, a Royal Navy fleet stationed off the coast of West Africa, was tasked with intercepting illegally trading slave ships. The African captives on board were 'liberated' and settled in Freetown, Sierra Leone.

In 1849, Captain Frederick Forbes of the HMS *Bonetta* was sent by Queen Victoria to persuade King Ghezo to cease trading in enslaved people. King Ghezo refused, but offered the captive girl Aina as a 'gift' to the Queen.

'She now passes by the name of "Sarah Bonetta" and is an intelligent, good tempered (I need hardly add Black) girl, about six or seven years of age'

Forbes took the girl Aina to Badagry, Nigeria, where the Church Missionary Society was establishing Christianity in West Africa through its churches and schools. The missionaries dressed Aina in traditional English Victorian clothing and baptised her Sarah Forbes Bonetta, giving her an English girl's first name and new last names from Captain Forbes and his ship. So began a new phase of the girl's life as an anglicised African.

Aina travelled with Forbes back to England, to be presented to Queen Victoria. What thoughts ran through the orphan girl's mind while on board that ship? What did she make of the sailors who taught her to speak English and tried to entertain her during the long journey?

On meeting Aina at Windsor Castle, Queen Victoria affirmed that she was 'graciously pleased to arrange for the education and subsequent fate of the child'. Aina would live with the Forbes family as a ward of the Queen, who described Aina in her diary as 'sharp and intelligent'.

Forbes noted in his own accounts that Aina was 'a perfect genius', adding that 'she has a great talent for music'. She was educated alongside the Forbes children, occasionally visiting the Queen at Windsor Castle to demonstrate her academic progress. This young girl, though far from her homeland, made an extraordinary impression on all those who met her, with her 'aptness of learning, and strength of mind and affection'.

In 1851, when Aina was around eight years old, she developed a persistent cough. The Queen, fearing that the English climate was harmful to Aina's health, consulted with Samuel Ajayi Crowther, a Krio bishop with the Church Missionary Society. Together, Bishop Crowther and Queen Victoria arranged for Aina to travel to Freetown. There she would attend the local Church Missionary School, and prepare for life as a missionary teacher. But as Aina was getting ready to set sail, the Forbes family received news that Captain Forbes had died at sea. This sudden bereavement must have made Aina's new journey even more daunting: in addition to the early loss of her own parents, she had now lost a guardian. Freetown was a port city on the coast of Sierra Leone, a country lush with green forests and blessed with white sandy beaches. A thriving city that was home to Fourah Bay College, a university established in 1827, Freetown was known as the 'Athens

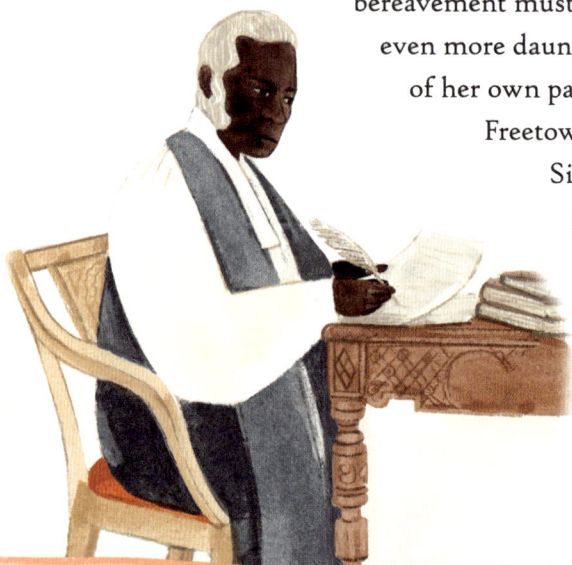

of Africa'. At the girls' school known as the Female Institution, Aina continued to be a brilliant student: in addition to studying Scripture and Prayer, she learned Arithmetic, Reading, Grammar and Geography. Musically talented, she excelled at the piano. Meanwhile Queen Victoria sent Aina gifts of books, games and toys, as well as money for clothing, paper and envelopes for letter-writing, and pomade to dress her hair.

Aina studied alongside girls from local communities, such as Krio, Kru and Mende. When she decided to throw a tea party for her friends in honour of the Queen's birthday, was she hoping to bring two different aspects of her life together?

After four years in Freetown, Aina returned to England at Queen Victoria's request. This time, she was placed in the care of the Schoen family in Gillingham, Kent. Reverend Schoen was a friend of the Queen's and a specialist in African languages. In her letters, Aina called Mrs Schoen 'Mama'.

In 1861, James Pinson Labulo Davies, a Yoruba businessman, asked Aina to marry him. She was hesitant: he was older than her, and a widower. In a letter to 'Mama' Schoen, Aina wrote, 'Am I to barter my peace of mind for money? No – never!' However, the Queen decided that the marriage should take place. So, in Brighton, on a rainy Thursday in August 1862, accompanied by cheers and umbrellas, and wreathed in orange blossoms, Aina and James were wed. Newspapers reported that the wedding party was made up of 'white ladies and African gentlemen, and African ladies and white gentlemen'.

The newlyweds travelled together to Freetown for James's trading affairs, and Aina taught at the school where she had been such a dedicated student. She returned to England once more when she became pregnant with her first daughter, Victoria, named for the Queen, who agreed to be the child's godmother. Letters reveal that Aina was to grow fonder of her husband as time passed. In 1868, she wrote to Mrs Schoen, 'The fact is that James is infinitely too good & kind to everybody...'

When Aina fell ill with tuberculosis, she settled in Funchal, Madeira, in the hope that the warm climate would ease her suffering. However, there was no hope of recovery, and in 1880 Aina died of her illness, leaving three children motherless.

In her extraordinary lifetime, Aina was photographed by the great society photographer of the age, Camille Silvy. The images of the young Yoruba woman in her Victorian dress are striking. Aina's poise and natural gravitas draw us into the portraits and compel us to consider her complex situation. An orphan taken from her community as a young child, she was given as a 'gift' to the most powerful woman in the world. Though she enjoyed many privileges, she was refused the power to make decisions governing her own life. Revered for her remarkable intelligence, she remained resilient. Aina survived, thrived, and wore multiple identities with ease: African princess, English gentlewoman, royal protégée and transatlantic traveller.

Samuel Coleridge-Taylor

(1875–1912)

COMPOSER, CONDUCTOR,
CAMPAIGNER

Samuel Coleridge-Taylor was born in Holborn, Central London, to Alice Martin, a young white English woman, and Daniel Hughes Taylor, a doctor from Freetown, Sierra Leone. Though Samuel grew up without his father, who may never have known of him, his African heritage became the lifeblood of his work.

Alice raised her son in Croydon, South London, with the help of her own mother Emily and her father Benjamin. When Samuel was five years old, Benjamin gave Samuel a violin and taught him to play. And when Samuel played, everyone listened.

This small shy boy had an outstanding gift for musical expression. His prodigious talent shone. Samuel's school headteacher recommended him to a local church choirmaster, who urged him to join the choir and surround himself with music. In 1890, Samuel became a student at the highly prestigious Royal College of Music.

As well as playing, Samuel loved writing his own music. Marvellous melodies wove their way through his lively mind like streaming ribbons in all colours of the rainbow. Out they flowed, the notes dancing through his hands into the violin, into the piano, into the written score. Impressed, Samuel's teachers offered him a scholarship to develop his talent on the violin. He accepted, but decided instead to study the art of composition.

College performances of Samuel's music illuminated his talent. He was spotted by the famous composer Edward Elgar, who recommended Samuel for a commission for the Three Choirs Festival. Elgar hailed Samuel as 'by far and away the cleverest fellow going amongst the young men'. Samuel's *Ballade in A Minor* for orchestra was performed at the Festival in September 1898. His star was on the rise.

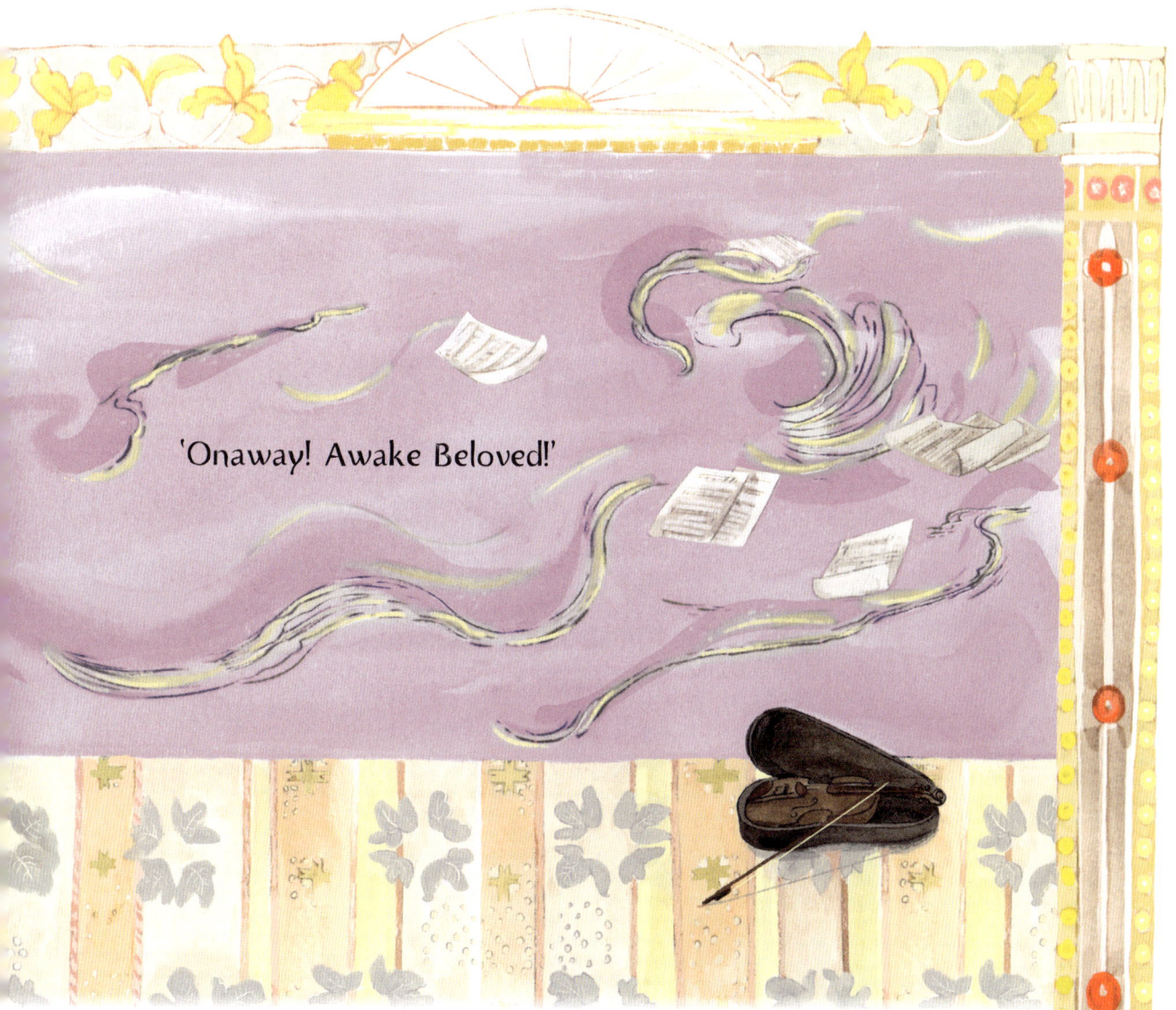

'Onaway! Awake Beloved!'

Named after the Romantic poet Samuel Taylor Coleridge, Samuel Coleridge-Taylor was inspired by literature and often set poems to music. He wrote a piece for solo voice and orchestra to the words of *Kubla Khan*, a poem written by his namesake.

Inspired by The Fisk Jubilee Singers, an African American spirituals choir who had toured Britain, Samuel infused his music with elements of African melodies and rhythms. He embedded his own cultural heritage in the classical tradition, saying: 'What Brahms has done for the Hungarian folk-music, Dvorak for the Bohemian, and Grieg for the Norwegian, I have tried to do for Negro Melodies'.

His most famous and enduring work was based on a poem by American poet Henry Wadsworth Longfellow. *The Song of Hiawatha* told the story of a Native American warrior, Hiawatha of the Ojibwe people. Into the main musical theme of the overture, or opening, Samuel wove the tune *Nobody Knows the Trouble I've Seen*, a famous African American spiritual song, thus drawing a link between the Native American and African American experience.

When celebrated African American poet Paul Laurence Dunbar visited London, a powerful partnership was born. The pair collaborated to create pieces such as *Dream Lovers*, *African Romances* and *African Suite*.

On 30 December 1899, just two days before the turn of the century, Samuel Coleridge-Taylor married Jessie Sarah Fleetwood Walmisley, a fellow student and pianist at the Royal College of Music. They had two children. Their son Hiawatha and their daughter Avril both grew up to become musical professionals.

Meanwhile, the new century ushered in a new phase of a key political movement. 'Pan-Africanism' held that all peoples of African descent – whether in Africa or across the diaspora – had common interests and should join together. From Pan-Africanism sprang a series of International Congresses, the Civil Rights Movement, and the African Union.

In 1900, the first ever Pan-African conference was held at Westminster Town Hall, London. The conference brought together delegates from across Africa, the Caribbean and America to campaign for Black liberation and African independence from colonising European nations. Samuel Coleridge-Taylor, inspired by his African heritage, was the youngest delegate to attend, and arranged the music for the momentous event.

Though they were not known to each other, Samuel had long been intrigued by his father and his cultural heritage. Daniel was a Sierra Leonean Krio, an ethnic group descended from liberated Africans who had settled in Freetown in the early nineteenth century. Now Samuel's Pan-African politics found artistic expression in the bars of his music.

His symphonic poem *Toussaint L'Ouverture* (1901) celebrated the life and legacy of the leader of the rebellion on the Caribbean island of Haiti. In 1791, the African Haitians had risen up against their French enslavers to claim their liberty and assert their national independence. In 1804, Haiti became the first independent state in the Caribbean and the first Black-led republic in the world. Samuel's rousing work was a clarion call for African self-governance and political liberation.

Samuel's Pan-African connections linked him to many esteemed cultural figures. Writer, philosopher and social activist W. E. B. Du Bois praised Samuel in his own work, holding him up as a shining example of Black excellence.

Samuel composed his own collection of Black spirituals: songs with swooping melodies, tinted with blue notes and tones, rich with yearning, sung from the soul. His exaltation of African American song inspired musicians in Washington, DC, to form the Samuel Coleridge-Taylor Choral Society. At their invitation, Samuel travelled to America in 1904, 1906 and 1910. He even met with the president, Theodore Roosevelt!

'It is well for us, O brother,
that you came so far to see us'

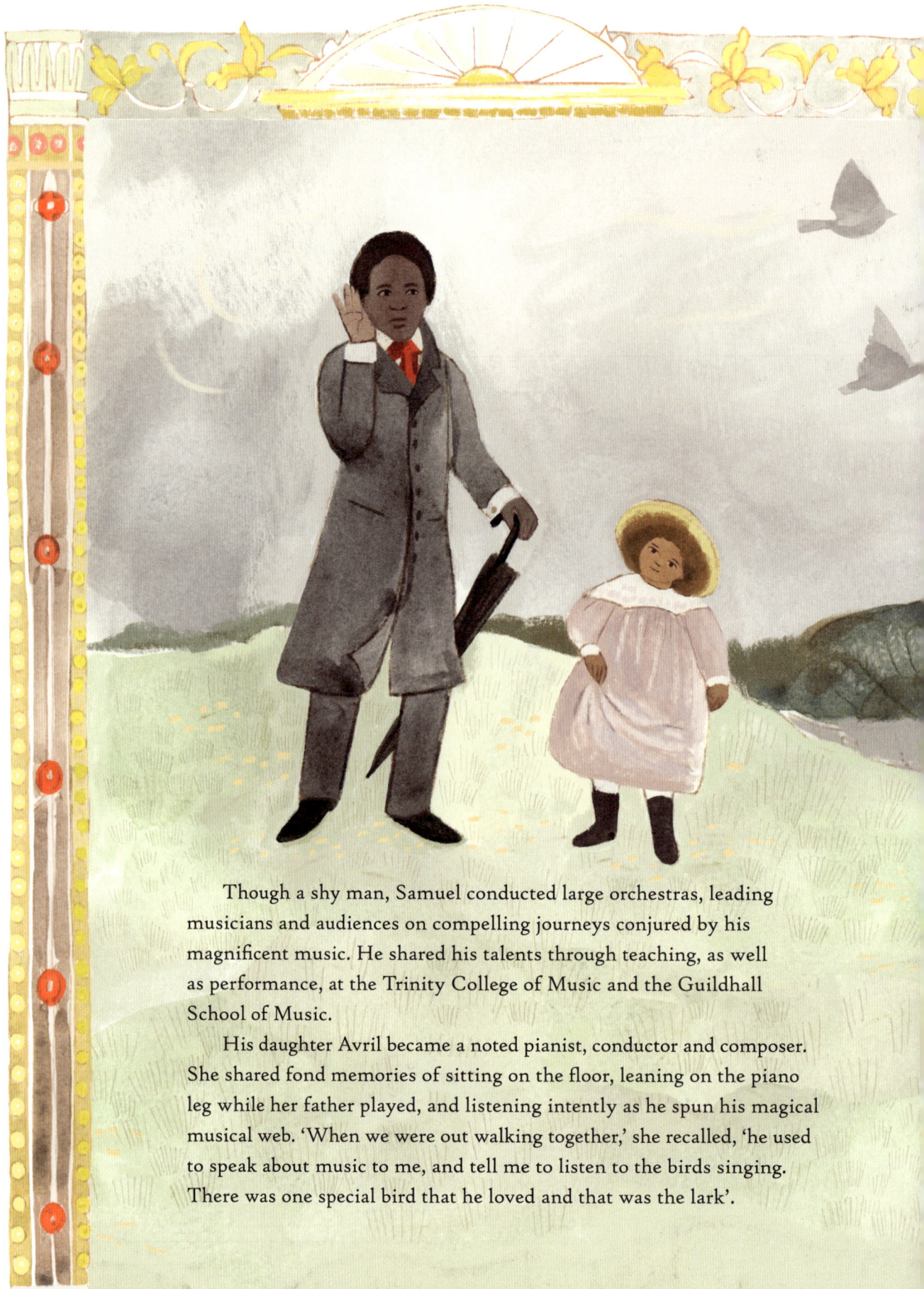

Though a shy man, Samuel conducted large orchestras, leading musicians and audiences on compelling journeys conjured by his magnificent music. He shared his talents through teaching, as well as performance, at the Trinity College of Music and the Guildhall School of Music.

His daughter Avril became a noted pianist, conductor and composer. She shared fond memories of sitting on the floor, leaning on the piano leg while her father played, and listening intently as he spun his magical musical web. 'When we were out walking together,' she recalled, 'he used to speak about music to me, and tell me to listen to the birds singing. There was one special bird that he loved and that was the lark'.

Sadly, Samuel's commitment to his craft and the demands of his stellar career led him to exhaustion. At the age of thirty-seven, he contracted pneumonia and died at his home in Croydon. Thousands of mourners attended his funeral. Samuel's headstone is inscribed with four bars of music from *The Song of Hiawatha*, and a quotation from his friend, the poet Alfred Noyes: 'Too young to die: his great simplicity, his happy courage in an alien world, his gentleness, made all that knew him love him'.

The Moderns

THE WORLD AT WAR

In the twentieth century, cataclysmic events – in the form of the First and the Second World Wars – shook the world to its very foundations. Alongside and intertwined with these shifts in global forces, campaigns for the rights of Black people all over the world developed and grew.

When World War One broke out in 1914, it became the largest and deadliest conflict the world had ever known. Over twenty million people lost their lives in a truly global war that spanned the continents of Africa and Asia as well as Europe. Volunteers from nations across the British Empire joined the fight, including men from the Caribbean, who were recruited into specially created regiments. Their contribution, however, went largely unacknowledged. Indeed, in 1919, when the war was over, and work for men was scarce, Black and Brown sailors returning to port cities in Britain came under attack from their white counterparts, as a series of race riots broke out in London, Liverpool, Hull, Cardiff, South Shields and Glasgow.

World War Two (1939–1945) was also fought on a global scale. Thousands of men and women of African and Caribbean heritage served, fought and died on Britain's behalf. But, in spite of the scale of this service and sacrifice, it would take a different kind of struggle for the contribution of Black people to British survival and success to be recognised.

THE BIRTH OF PAN-AFRICANISM

In the wake of the 1884 Berlin Conference (see p. 63), the growing population of African and Caribbean students and professionals in Britain had begun to form political alliances. They organised in order to challenge colonialism, and to fight for the freedom and independence of their nations from imperial power. Alongside these political movements grew campaigns for civil rights for Black people in Britain.

In July 1900, the first ever Pan-African Conference was held in London, organised by Trinidadian lawyer and activist Henry Sylvester Williams. Leaders and representatives from nations all over the world came together to discuss their common goals of self-government and equal rights for all. Several Pan-African Congresses would follow, including Paris (1919), London (1921 and 1923), New York (1927), and Manchester (1945). At the Congress in Manchester, a clarion call was issued for racial discrimination to be outlawed. The Congress's 'Challenge to the Colonial Powers' was instrumental in securing independence for African nations, including Ghana and Kenya: 'We are determined to be free. We want education. We want the right to earn a decent living; the right to express our thoughts and emotions, to adopt and create forms of beauty'.

RESISTANCE, STRUGGLE, PROGRESS

This call for equal rights in the fields of education, employment, and intellectual and artistic expression neatly encapsulates the myriad struggles of Britain's Black population over the centuries. In the twentieth century, through powerful combinations of resistance, action, voice, community, art and joy, Black British people persisted in finding new ways to forge their own paths to personal and political freedom.

Harold Moody

(1882–1947)

DOCTOR, PREACHER, CIVIL RIGHTS LEADER

Dr Harold Moody was a committed campaigner for the rights of Black people in Britain and all over the world. Born in 1882 in Kingston, Jamaica, he was the eldest child of six. His parents, Charles and Christine, ran a successful pharmacy. Harold worked hard at school. As a teenager, his Christian beliefs began to shape his ideas about humanity and race, forming the bedrock of his future work. Later in life, his stirring speeches as an activist would echo his powerful preaching from the pulpit.

In 1904, Harold travelled to Britain to study medicine at King's College, London. He graduated with flying colours and was awarded academic prizes for his outstanding work. However, when he applied for a job at King's College Hospital, he was refused on account of his colour. The 'Colour Bar', a practice of racial discrimination, was used to deny Black people access to jobs and housing, and entrance into restaurants, theatres and hotels. While not enshrined in law, it was common practice in Britain throughout the first half of the twentieth century. Harold's personal experiences of repeatedly being denied work and accommodation spurred him into action. The Colour Bar had to be confronted and dismantled.

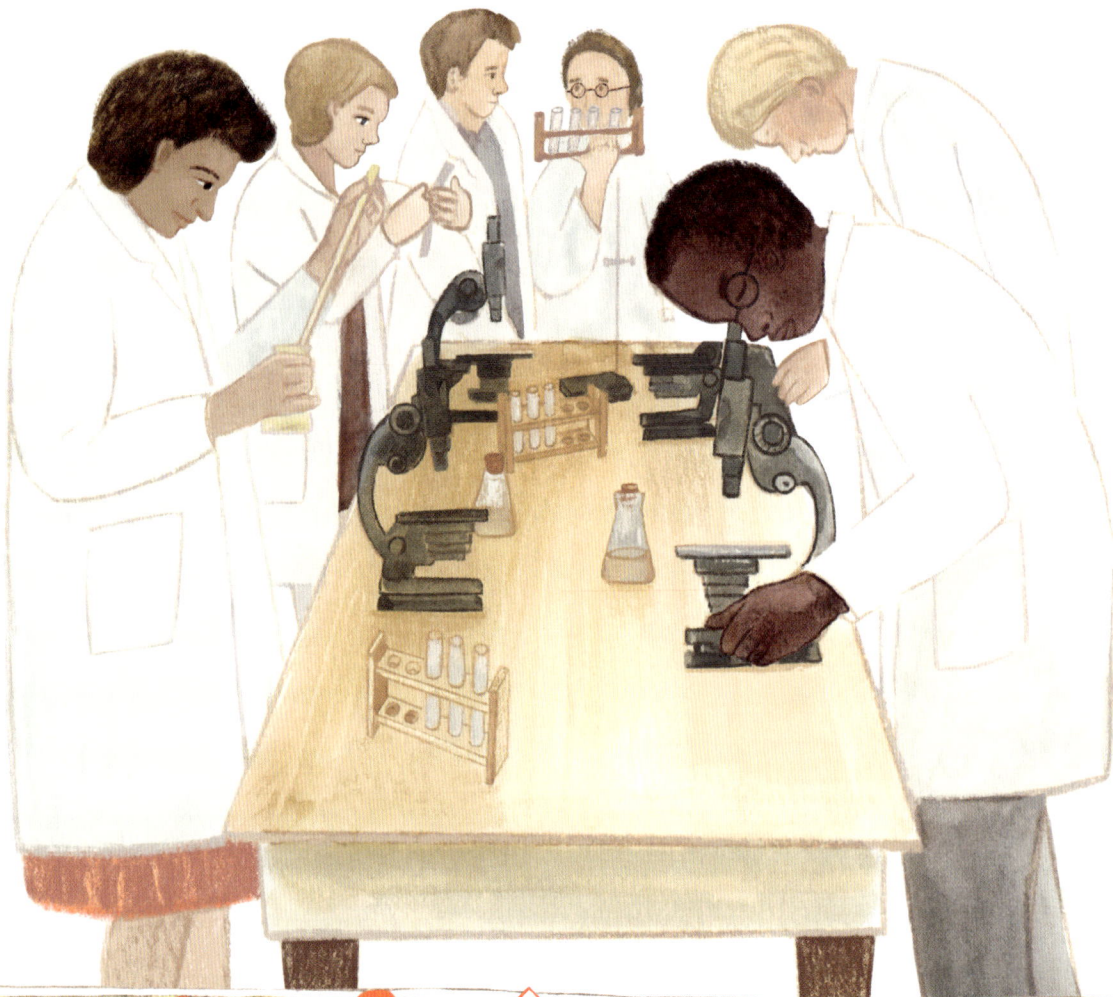

In 1913, Harold finally found a home in Peckham. Determined to work, he set up his own GP practice there. In the years before the NHS, doctors' surgeries run by individuals offered crucial services for the local community. Harold treated everyone who came to him, whether they could pay him or not. In the same year, he married Olive Mabel Tranter, a white English nurse whom he had met while studying at King's. The couple ran the surgery together and themselves became parents to six children.

In 1922, the Moodys moved to a new house in Queen's Road, Peckham. It soon became a safe haven for travelling Black people in need of a meal or somewhere to stay. A man committed to his community, Harold offered shelter, sustenance, and practical advice to people experiencing racial discrimination.

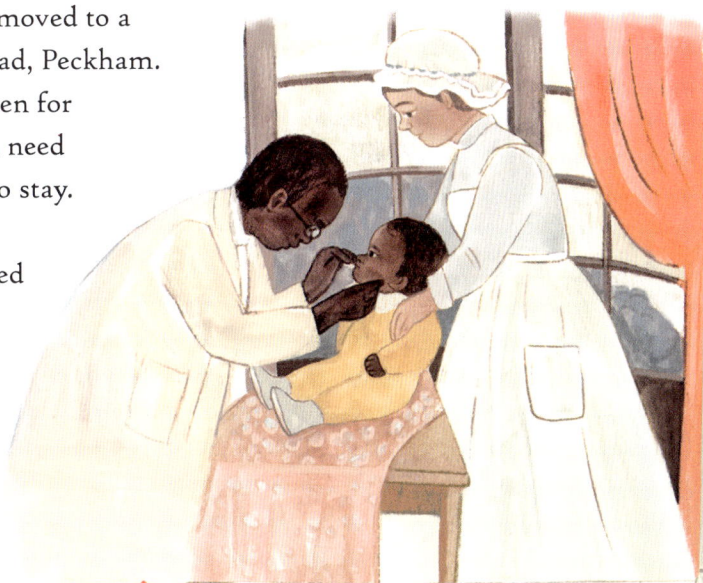

In the years following World War One, many Black nurses and medical students lived in London. After serving the war effort, they had been promised jobs in hospitals. When these promises were not kept, they sought help from Harold. African and African Caribbean graduates and professionals who had been refused jobs in the Army also came to him for advice. Harold campaigned directly on people's behalf, taking up individual cases with employers, landlords and business owners.

Harold realised that there was strength in numbers. Now it was time to form an organisation to push for change and to secure civil rights for Black people in Britain and beyond. Over the years, Harold had built up a network of like-minded colleagues: doctors, lawyers, educators, journalists and politicians from across Britain, Africa, the Caribbean and the United States. In March 1931, at a meeting at the YMCA on Tottenham Court Road, London, the League of Coloured Peoples was born.

The League – known as the LCP – was a humanitarian organisation with Pan-African politics. It set out 'to promote and protect the social, educational, economic and political interests of its members'. The LCP worked to raise awareness of the welfare of Black people all over the world; to improve race relations; to co-operate with other Black-led organisations; to help Black people in financial need.

Harold often used his own money for the latter. A charitable man, he organised Christmas parties and summer outings for the children of working families. Boys and girls who rarely, if ever, got to leave the city were treated to a bus ride to the rolling hills and fields of Epsom Downs. There, they could play freely in the fresh air of the English countryside.

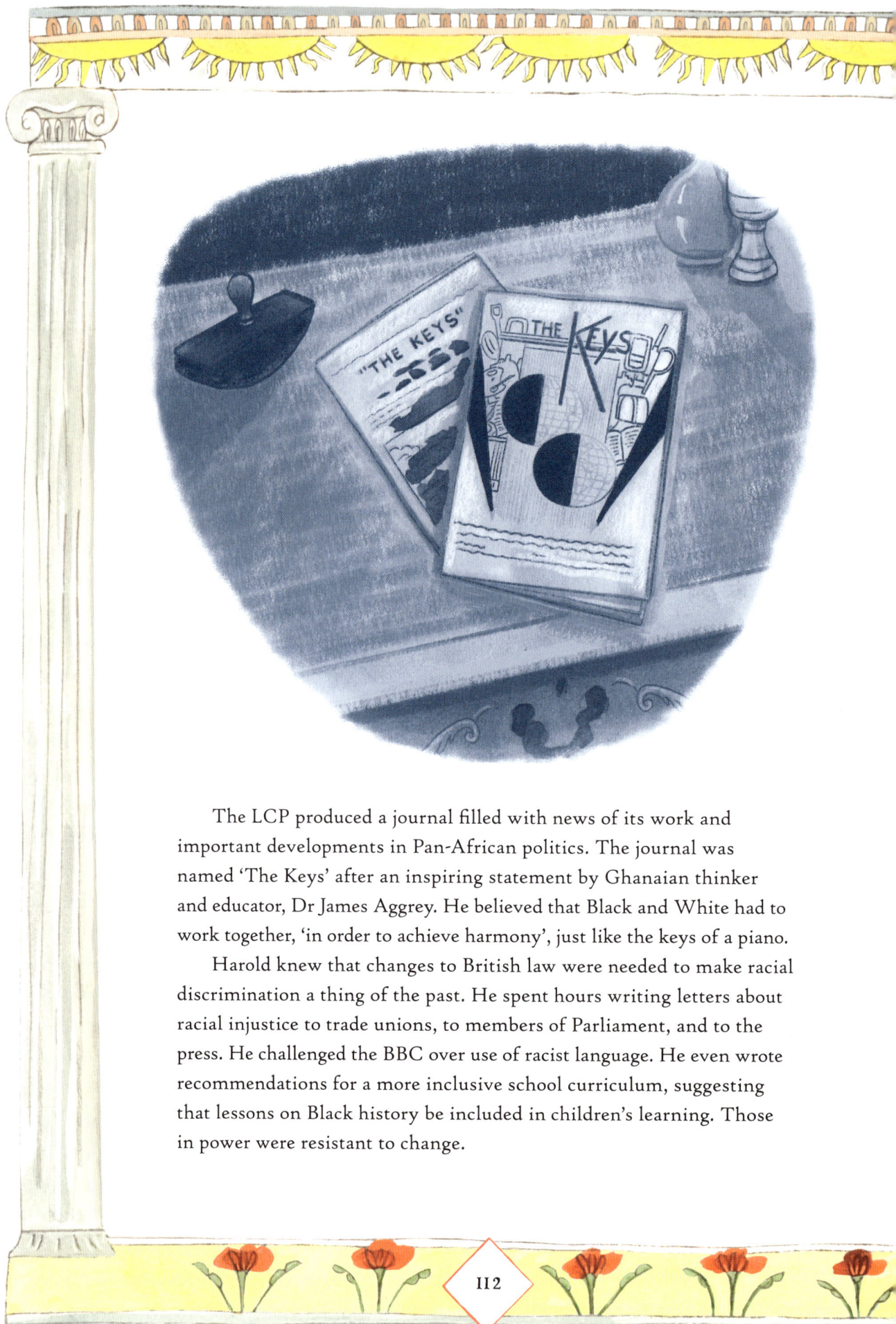

The LCP produced a journal filled with news of its work and important developments in Pan-African politics. The journal was named 'The Keys' after an inspiring statement by Ghanaian thinker and educator, Dr James Aggrey. He believed that Black and White had to work together, 'in order to achieve harmony', just like the keys of a piano.

Harold knew that changes to British law were needed to make racial discrimination a thing of the past. He spent hours writing letters about racial injustice to trade unions, to members of Parliament, and to the press. He challenged the BBC over use of racist language. He even wrote recommendations for a more inclusive school curriculum, suggesting that lessons on Black history be included in children's learning. Those in power were resistant to change.

Meanwhile, politics on the world stage were shifting drastically. During the 1930s, far-right Fascism was spreading across Europe. When the Italian dictator Mussolini invaded Abyssinia (now Ethiopia) in 1935, Pan-African organisations all over the world raised money and sent support to the Ethiopian people. Their leader, Emperor Haile Selassie, came to Britain, where he was met by the Jamaican writer Una Marson (see p. 136), a key member of the LCP. Italy's troops were finally defeated in East Africa in 1941. Ethiopia and Liberia remain the only two African countries never to have been colonised.

When World War Two broke out, thousands of African and African Caribbean men and women served in the armed forces, both in Britain and around the world. But the Army still had laws preventing people of colour from holding positions of command. Harold persuaded the War Office to change its legislation. Five of his own children went on to be commissioned by the Army or Air Force as officers, his son Harold and daughter Christine as army doctors.

Many Black people also served in the Blitz as fire wardens, air-raid wardens, stretcher-bearers or first-aid workers. When a rocket explosion in New Cross, South London, killed almost two hundred people and injured many more, Harold was immediately on the scene, working through the day and night to clear the bomb damage and treat injured people from his local community.

In 1944 the LCP drew up a 'Charter for Coloured Peoples', demanding self-government for people in African and Caribbean colonies. The Charter also urged that racial discrimination in employment or in public spaces be made illegal.

Harold continued to campaign towards these goals until his death from influenza in 1947. Sadly, without his leadership, the LCP dwindled, surviving for only a few more years. However, 1965 finally saw the first in a series of Race Relations Acts, outlawing overt racial discrimination. These laws have direct roots in the work of Harold Arundel Moody, the committed doctor and community activist. He made it his life's work to challenge racial prejudice, to devise solutions for social problems, and to lead his fellow human beings in the fight for their civil rights.

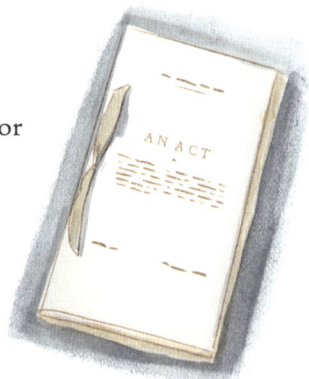

Walter Tull

(1888–1918)

A FOOTBALL CHAMPION
AND WAR HERO

Walter Tull was born in 1888 in Folkestone, Kent, to Daniel Tull, a Barbadian carpenter, and Alice Palmer, a white English farm worker. Daniel's parents, William Criss and Anna Lashly, had been born into enslavement in Barbados. After slavery was abolished in 1833, William and Anna were forced to continue to work for no pay during the four-year period of 'apprenticeship'. William decided to reject the surname of his so-called master Criss and was baptised William Tull in 1836. He took the name Tull from three signatures he had seen on an 1823 petition calling for rights for Black Barbadians.

Even after emancipation, under British rule, conditions were very harsh for many Black Barbadians. There were few employment opportunities, and wages for available work were low. In 1876 Daniel left for the island of St Lucia, and after three years there, he secured a passage as a ship's carpenter to England. He landed at Folkestone.

A literate, skilled, churchgoing man, Daniel settled quickly into his new community. He married Alice and they had six children together: Bertha (who sadly died in infancy), William, Cecilia, Edward, Walter and Elsie.

When Walter was seven years old, his mother died of cancer. The family were devastated. Daniel knew that the children were at risk of being taken into the Folkestone workhouse if there was no one to look after them while he worked. He swiftly married again – this time to Alice's niece, Clara – so that the children could be looked after. A year into his second marriage, and just three months after the birth of his seventh child,

Daniel died suddenly
of heart disease. Clara
felt she could not cope alone
with the children and arrangements
were made for Walter and his brother
Edward to be sent to the National Children's
Home and Orphanage in Bethnal Green, East London.

Walter and Edward loved each other very dearly. They stayed close during their time at the orphanage and looked out for one another. For solace, they sang together in the orphanage choir. They joined the choir on a national tour, singing in cities and towns all over Britain. During their time in Glasgow, Edward was selected for adoption by a new family. The loving brothers were to be separated, losing their final family tie.

Now bereft of his closest companion, Walter threw himself into playing football for the orphanage team. He was an impressive midfield player, with awe-inspiring tackling and passing skills. Visiting scouts soon spotted him and he won a trial with Clapton FC. Within months, he was playing for their first team. His outstanding sportsmanship and gentle manner earned him high praise from the press.

In 1909, he was signed by Tottenham Hotspur, already a prestigious club on the rise. This was a turning point in Walter's career. At a time when few people voyaged around the world, he accompanied the club on an international tour, travelling to South America to play in Argentina and Uruguay.

But back home, the shadow of racism still loomed. At a Tottenham away game versus Bristol City, Walter was subjected to racial abuse from a hostile crowd of opponents. The *Football Star* reporter wrote:

'Let me tell those Bristol hooligans that Tull is so clean in mind and method as to be a model for all white men who play football'. Uncertain of how to confront the public abuse Walter received, Tottenham moved him to the reserve bench.

'Tull was the best forward on the field'

Keen for more opportunities to shine on the football field, Walter signed with Northampton FC in 1911. His game went from strength to strength. He played in over a hundred matches and earned himself a reputation as a calm footballer and an excellent team player. Interest in this exceptional role model was high. The Glasgow football team, Rangers, offered him a contract. Playing for them would open up the opportunity for Walter to join his beloved brother Edward in Glasgow. But it was not to be.

In 1914, the British Empire entered World War One, the most brutal theatre of war the world had known to date. The War Office and the Football Association recruited professional footballers into a Football Battalion to persuade more young men to follow their lead and fight in France. Walter enlisted immediately. A natural leader, he was promoted quickly through the Army ranks. Walter fought on the front line, where men lived, slept and ate in mud trenches – ditches dug out of the ground – ridden with rats and lice. Artillery shells dropped from the sky, blasting to pieces the ground where they fell. Cannons rumbled constantly, punctuated by the patter of rapid machine-gun fire.

In 1916, Walter was caught up in the devastating trench warfare of the Battle of the Somme, which resulted in over a million casualties. Like so many thousands of soldiers, Walter was shattered by shell shock – post-traumatic stress disorder induced by warfare. He was sent home to England to recover.

When he was considered fit enough to fight again, Walter was posted to Scotland and recommended for officer training on account of his bravery. This was in spite of British military laws banning any person of colour or 'not of pure European descent' from becoming an officer. These laws would later be challenged and overturned by civil rights activist Harold Moody (see p. 106).

Having become the first Black officer in the British Army, Walter was posted as a second lieutenant to Italy, where he led his men into battle at Piave. Just months later, while crossing 'no man's land' at the Second Battle of the Somme, on 25 March 1918, Walter was killed by a machine-gun bullet to the head. The men under his command tried three times to bring his body back from the battlefield so that he could be buried, but they were driven back by enemy fire. Walter's body was never retrieved. He was twenty-nine years old.

After his death, Walter's commanding officer said: 'His courage was of a high order and was combined with a quiet unassuming manner'. Edward Tull, who had been forced to part company from his beloved brother all those years ago, said that reading the telegram announcing Walter's death was 'the worst moment of my life'.

In his brief lifetime, Walter Tull moved the hearts and minds of many. Though he started life in a loving family home, his early childhood was wracked by grief and loss. He spent years in a care home, separated from his siblings, yet still managed to survive and thrive. As a footballer, he showed outstanding skill and grace. In battle, his bravery and his natural but gentle leadership style earned him the respect and admiration of his fellow soldiers. More than a century after his passing, he continues to inspire.

Hundreds of thousands of Black soldiers fought in World War One. Some, like Walter, were Black Englishmen enlisted into standard regiments. But the Army also recruited troops from across the globe, drafting in soldiers from colonies in the British Empire. The British West Indies Regiment, for example, was established in 1915 for volunteers from the Caribbean. For decades, however, Black soldiers were not included in victory parades or events commemorating the war. It would be many years before their contribution would be acknowledged.

Evelyn Dove
(1902–1987)

INTERNATIONAL ENTERTAINER
AND SINGER OF SPIRITUALS

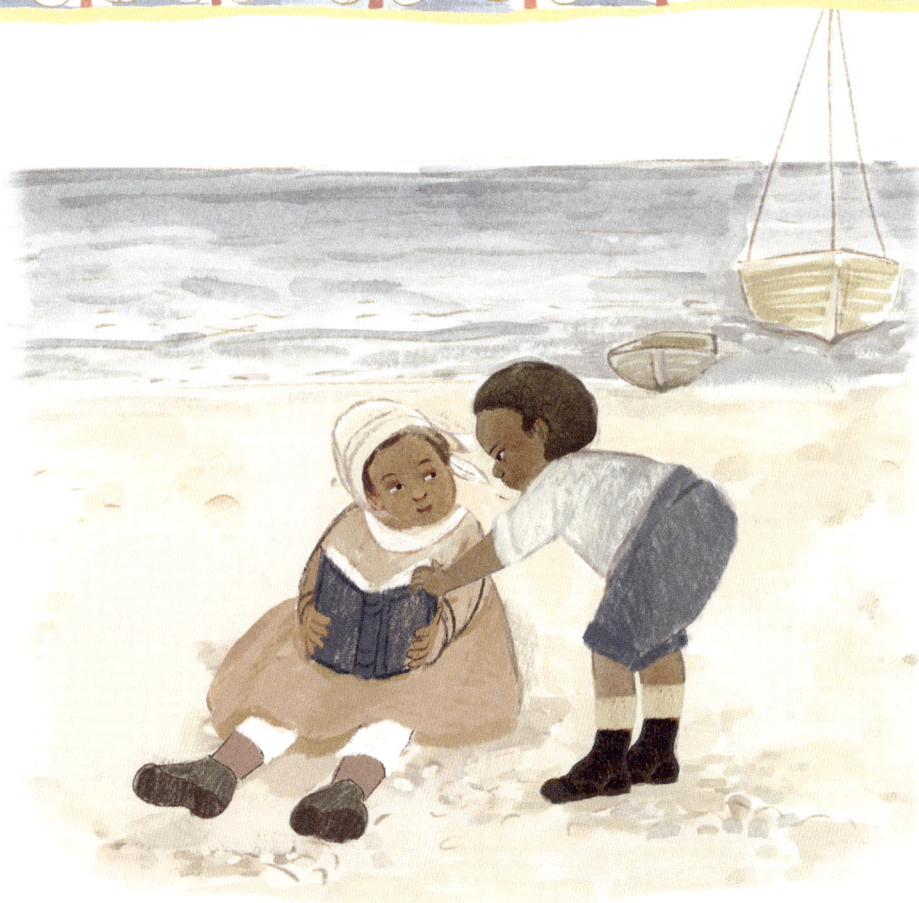

Evelyn Dove was born in 1902 at the Lying-in Hospital, Endell Street, Covent Garden, to an English mother, Augusta Dove (née Winchester), and a Sierra Leonean father, Frans Dove, a barrister. During Evelyn's early childhood, the family lived in Battersea, South London. When Frans and Augusta divorced in 1920, Augusta moved the family to Hove, near Brighton, in her home county of Sussex.

Frans was one of several elite West Africans living and working in Edwardian England. He travelled regularly between London, Freetown in Sierra Leone, and Accra in Ghana, practising law and trading. Evelyn and her brother Frank were both privately educated: she at Cheltenham Ladies' College, he at Cranleigh. Like his sister, Frank would go on to make his mark on the world. He studied law at Oxford, fought in World War One, and represented Britain as a boxer in the 1920 Olympics.

At the age of fifteen, Evelyn joined the Royal Academy of Music to study piano, singing and elocution. She loved classical music and longed to be an opera singer. Her warm contralto voice impressed her teachers, and by the time she graduated from the school in 1919 she had been awarded bronze and silver medals for her singing.

That same year she married Milton Alphonso Luke, a Trinidadian student who had served in the British West Indies Regiment during World War One (see p. 125). This would be the first of three marriages.

1919 was a tumultuous year for Black communities in Britain. Black men who had served in the war had returned to a fight for jobs and simmering racial hostility. Port cities such as London, Liverpool, Cardiff and Newcastle saw heated race riots as Black and Brown men were attacked in the streets and in their homes. Similarly, America was experiencing a 'Red Summer': a period of sustained racist attacks on Black communities and African American soldiers returning home from the war. On both sides of the Atlantic, the need for organised demands for civil rights was growing.

Amid these tensions, something else was brewing in America that would shake the music world to its foundations and change the course of music forever. An exciting musical form was bubbling and bursting out from cities such as New Orleans, Chicago and New York. In clubs, bars and theatres, Black musicians were inventing and playing brand new, bold, brash sounds. Jazz was on the rise.

Led by African American violinist and composer Will Marion Cook, the Southern Syncopated Orchestra was a jazz band of Black musicians from West Africa, the Caribbean and the United States. When the SSO arrived in Britain in 1919, they brought jazz to British shores. Evelyn joined the band as a pianist and vocalist, singing a rich repertoire of spirituals and upbeat melodies alongside classical compositions by Samuel Coleridge-Taylor (see p. 94).

Brimming with excitement and hope, the SSO embarked on a grand tour of Europe. This sophisticated syncopated band played to packed theatres and received rave reviews. But on 9 October 1921, the ship they were sailing on, the SS *Rowan*, collided with an American steamer off the coast of Glasgow. Veiled in thick fog, the *Rowan* was struck by a third ship and was cut clean in two. It sank within minutes, and nine members of the band lost their lives at sea. Evelyn was one of the survivors. Eyewitness accounts said that she sang spirituals from a life-raft to comfort people in distress as they awaited rescue from the freezing ocean. According to Pathé News, she even saved the life of one of her fellow band members.

The orchestra disbanded within weeks of the accident, but some of its surviving members formed new groups to keep its sound alive. Evelyn teamed up with a small group of ex-SSO musicians to sing spirituals at prestigious venues in London. In 1925 she left England to travel Europe, singing and dancing on stage in revue shows and cabarets. But shows performed by all-Black casts designed for white-only audiences were often constrained by racial stereotypes: Black performers were presented as one-dimensional characters, either happy-go-lucky or beset by constant blues.

It was as a solo artist that Evelyn felt she could really shine, and she performed to rapturous audiences in cabaret performances in Germany, Denmark, Italy, France and India. When the celebrated African American star Josephine Baker left Paris to go on tour, Evelyn was invited to fill her spot at the legendary Casino de Paris.

'An artist of international reputation, one of the leading personalities of Europe's entertainment world'

Meanwhile, in New York, as collective Black consciousness was growing, a thrilling new arts movement bloomed: the Harlem Renaissance. Black musicians, dancers, artists, writers and thinkers were taking New York by storm in a creative outpouring of cultural expression and experimentation. And jazz was its music. In 1935, Evelyn was invited to appear at Connie's Inn, a famous club where jazz and blues stars such as Billie Holiday, Bessie Smith and Louis Armstrong had all performed.

But ultimately Evelyn still yearned to be an opera singer. She felt that in America her opportunities were limited by attitudes to her colour. And racial segregation in public spaces meant that Black audiences were often not allowed to enter the clubs that played Black music. Disillusioned with what America had to offer, Evelyn returned home.

In Britain, radio was seizing the hearts of the nation, broadcasting to listeners since the birth of the BBC in 1922. The launch of the BBC's 'Empire Service' in 1932 meant that listeners in British colonies all over the world could tune in. Demand for Black music was at a peak, and Evelyn secured a regular singing spot on the airwaves.

When World War Two broke out in 1939, performers were invited to entertain the troops to help boost their morale. Evelyn sang at special concerts for armed forces all over the country. On the radio, and in person, Evelyn's soft, soulful voice soothed people's hearts and minds amidst the chaos and tragedy of the war.

In 1945, Evelyn was paired with Trinidadian singer and actor Edric Connor for a music programme called *Serenade in Sepia*. Evelyn and Edric were a golden combination: their talent and charisma made the show such a roaring success that the BBC turned it into a television programme. Images of Evelyn and Edric were beamed out to viewers from the iconic television studios at Alexandra Palace in North London.

In the 1950s, Edric and his wife Pearl established a theatre agency, offering a vital network for Black and Brown actors in Britain. In 1961, they set up the Negro Theatre Workshop, a company aiming to promote the work of African and Caribbean playwrights. Evelyn performed in several theatre productions, including a stage adaptation of Alan Paton's famous anti-apartheid novel *Cry, the Beloved Country*, and in *The Dark Disciples*, a blues-inspired version of St Luke's Gospel. In her middle

years, Evelyn now embraced a new kind of performance: powerfully political storytelling on stage, in community with fellow actors.

These moments in Evelyn's stage career would be her last. In the years that followed, isolated and alone, she fell ill. Evelyn spent the final decade of her life in a nursing home in Surrey, where she died in 1987. Only a handful of recordings of her exquisite voice survive: testament to the true talent of an intriguing and illustrious entertainer.

Una Marson

(1905–1965)

FEMINIST, JOURNALIST, ACTIVIST

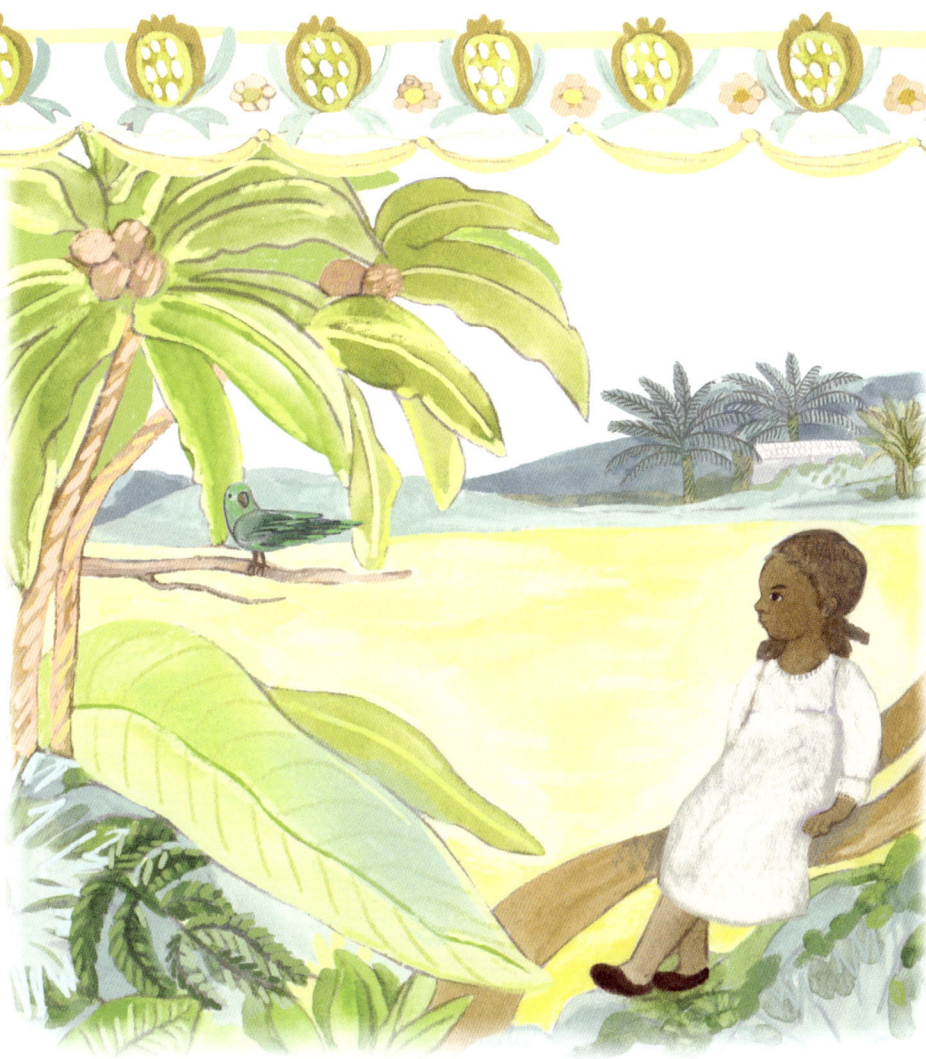

Una Maud Victoria Marson was born on 6 February 1905 to Reverend Solomon Isaac Marson and Ada Marson in Sharon, a village in the parish of St Ann's, Jamaica. She grew up in a large and lively household, with her parents, her nine siblings – three of whom were adopted – and her grandmother Rosalind, who helped to raise the children.

Una won a scholarship to a girls' boarding school, where she was educated in a traditional English style. She immersed herself in poetry such as William Wordsworth's ballads, celebrating the beauty of nature. As a young girl, Una was captivated by the splendour of Jamaica's landscape and felt compelled to explore the feelings it inspired in her. Even in her early girlhood she was already writing poetry, crafting free expression of her innermost thoughts and emotions on the page.

When Una was only eleven years old, her beloved father died. Her mother and her sisters moved to the bustling capital city of Kingston, and Una joined them there when her schooling was over. Now that her father was dead, Una felt a sense of duty towards her mother, and trained as a stenographer – a professional typist – so that she could quickly secure a job.

Una's first jobs were with the Salvation Army and the YMCA, charitable organisations dedicated to helping Jamaicans living in extreme poverty due to low wages and high unemployment under colonial rule. Una's burgeoning sense of social justice infused her work when she became assistant editor of a political monthly journal called *The Critic*. Here she began to spread her wings as a writer.

Determined to do more with her voice, at the age of just twenty-three, Una set up a new monthly magazine for women called *The Cosmopolitan*. The year was 1928 and this was a women's magazine with a difference. As the first Jamaican woman to edit a publication, Una brought the lives, experiences and opinions of Jamaican women centre stage. *The Cosmopolitan* encouraged debate and celebrated culture, covering subjects ranging from women's working conditions to Jamaican poetry. In an early editorial, Una wrote, 'This is the age of woman: whatever man has done, women may do'. Una Marson was coming into her own as a feminist writer.

In 1930 she published her first volume of poetry, *Tropic Reveries*, and was praised in the *Jamaica Times* for her 'fine talent'. She published three more volumes of poems: *Heights and Depths*, *The Moth and the Star*, and *Towards the Stars*. Some poems celebrated the majesty of the Jamaican landscape; others wittily challenged racism and sexism. Una called her poems 'heart-throbs'. Writing in a range of voices, including her own national patois, and drawing on her own experiences, Una wrote fiercely political poems alongside blues poems and lyrics singing the joys and pains of love.

But poetry was not to be the only channel for her creative impulses. Una had been captivated by the theatre since girlhood. In 1932, her first play, *At What a Price*, was staged in Kingston. This brought public acclaim and earned her enough money to buy herself a ticket to sail to Britain.

On her arrival in London, Una headed straight to 164 Queen's Road in Peckham, where Jamaican doctor and civil rights activist Harold Moody and his family welcomed travelling compatriots into their home with open arms (see p. 106). Harold was the leader of the League of Coloured Peoples (LCP), an anti-racist organisation. Students from Africa and the Caribbean stayed in his home, debated politics, and worked together to improve living and working conditions for Black and Brown people. Una's room 'looked out on to a grass tennis court and the colourful, rose-filled garden'. Here, she found comfort, companionship and community.

Life in London, however, brought daily experiences of racism. White children called her names in the street – insults which Una would consider at length in her poetry. Work was also hard to find. Though Una was trained as a professional secretary, she was rejected repeatedly when she applied for jobs, in spite of her excellent references – and people were prepared to tell her why. Una was experiencing the effects of the 'Colour Bar' that Harold Moody and his colleagues were fighting to dismantle.

Una joined the struggle. She became a key member of the LCP and dedicated herself to campaigning for the rights of people of colour – and women, in particular – all over the world. A skilled and experienced journalist, she became editor of *The Keys*, the LCP publication. Una also joined the International Alliance of Women for Suffrage and Equal Citizenship. When the Italian dictator Benito Mussolini

invaded Abyssinia, Emperor Haile Selassie travelled to Europe to seek support from the League of Nations. Una met him in London and accompanied him to a convention in Geneva. She thus became the first Black woman to be invited to attend the League of Nations, and successfully added her voice to the fight for Abyssinian freedom.

In 1936, Una returned to Jamaica to promote Jamaican literature and explore her love of theatre. She was one of the founding members of the Kingston Readers and Writers Club and the Kingston Drama Club. She collaborated with the ebullient Jamaican spoken-word poet Louise Bennett – 'Miss Lou' – on a new play called *London Calling*. Una's 1938 drama, *Pocomania*, tackled the tensions between traditional African rituals and the new middle-class Christian way of life in Jamaica. Meanwhile she continued with her social work, founding the Jamaica 'Save the Children' fund, to improve access to education.

As London fell prey to the Blitz during World War Two, Londoners relied on the radio for support and solace. In 1941, Una got a job at the BBC as an assistant on *Calling the West Indies*, a radio programme that invited Caribbean servicemen and women in Britain to send messages over the airwaves to family and friends in their home islands. Una demonstrated confidence and panache as a broadcaster. Impressed and intrigued, the writer George Orwell – author of *Animal Farm* and, later, *1984* – invited her to contribute to a literature programme called *Voice*.

Una created a new strand called *Caribbean Voices*, a showcase of Caribbean writers, bringing their poetry, drama and fiction to new audiences. The programme helped to establish a thriving Caribbean literary scene in Britain, launching the careers of writers who had settled in London, such as Sam Selvon of Trinidad, George Lamming of Barbados, and Andrew Salkey of Jamaica.

Sadly, Una's last years were dogged by exhaustion, both physical and emotional. She died in hospital in Kingston, in 1965, aged just sixty. Yet her literary legacy shines on. Una's plays place a woman's perspective at the centre of pressing political stories. Her powerful poetry sings in a range of registers to explore the triumphs and challenges of Black women's lives in Britain and the Caribbean.

Una dedicated her life to effecting social change, both in her home country of Jamaica and across the globe. It is believed that she wrote her own life story, *The Autobiography of a Brown Girl*, but a manuscript has not yet been found. Perhaps one day we will have the chance to read about Una Marson's life in her own words.

Claudia Jones

(1915–1964)

POLITICAL CAMPAIGNER,
CARNIVAL PIONEER

Claudia Jones was born Claudia Vera Cumberbatch on 21
February 1915, in Port-of-Spain, Trinidad. Financial difficulties
following World War One prompted her parents to move
to New York in 1922. Claudia and her sisters followed two years later,
joining their parents in Harlem, the district where African Americans
and African Caribbeans lived side by side in community. In Harlem,
grassroots politics thrived on street corners where people persuasively
spoke truth to power. While Black cultural expression was blossoming
in the Harlem Renaissance (see p. 133), Black consciousness movements –
such as the Universal Negro Improvement Association, led by Jamaican
political leader Marcus Garvey – were growing and gathering support.

Claudia excelled at school. She worked hard, was elected Mayor of the School Council, and was awarded a prize for good citizenship. But poverty created punishing living conditions for many families in Harlem. The apartment Claudia's family lived in was cramped, cold and damp. Claudia's mother, a garment worker, died suddenly in 1927 of spinal meningitis, brought on by exhaustion and overwork. Claudia developed tuberculosis of the lung: a respiratory disease that would hound her for life. When she was seventeen, her poor health placed her in hospital for a year. She later wrote that this gave her 'an opportunity to read avidly, to think deeply, about the social ideas instilled in me by my mother and father'.

Claudia's growing interest in politics led her to follow current affairs closely. She began writing for a Harlem journal, and soon had her own column called 'Claudia's Comments'. She joined the National Association for the Advancement of Colored People, which was fast becoming a crucial organisation in the fight for civil rights.

In 1936 Claudia joined the youth section of the Communist Party and began writing editorials for their newspaper, the *Daily Worker*. There, her column 'Half the World' focused on tackling women's oppression. While growing into her socialist and feminist politics, she was sharpening her writing skills and developing an expert editorial eye.

Also a charismatic speaker, Claudia addressed crowds in Madison Square Garden, highlighting injustices and setting out solutions. In 1949 she published an essay called 'An End to the Neglect of the Problems of the Negro Woman!' – a clear clarion call to confront racial and gender inequality for working Black women.

The US government responded with suspicion and hostility. In the years following the end of World War Two, along with other Communist activists and writers, Claudia was harassed continually by federal agents and arrested repeatedly on false charges of plotting to overthrow the government.

In 1953, alongside twelve colleagues, she was sentenced to a year and a day in prison, and she was to be sent out of the country permanently afterwards. On her release from prison in December 1955, a farewell party was held in a Harlem hotel. Three hundred and fifty friends and supporters attended. Her close friend, the actor and activist Paul Robeson, gave a speech in her honour, saying: 'In her dedicated work and leadership Claudia has given new life to the finest traditions of our country ... the struggle for Negro liberation, for women's rights, for human dignity and fulfilment'.

Claudia left the USA for Britain, forbidden to return to the USA or to Trinidad. She settled in London, initially knowing no one, forced to nurture new networks of friends and colleagues. She joined the British Communist Party, but they did not welcome Claudia and her confident voice. She would need to find other ways to turn her political beliefs into action.

Meanwhile, Britain's Black population was growing. African and Caribbean men and women had fought and served on behalf of Britain in World War Two. When the war was over, some stayed to work in jobs promised to them in return for their war service. Others returned home to the Caribbean until they were invited back to help re-build a broken nation. The birth of the National Health Service in Britain in 1948 meant that doctors, nurses, dentists and other health workers were needed. The British government recruited people directly from British colonies in Africa and the Caribbean to do crucial work in hospitals, in construction in transport services. In June 1948, the SS *Windrush* was one of many ships bringing Black people with British citizenship from the Caribbean to Britain.

Claudia recognised that a newspaper was needed for Caribbeans living in Britain to share and discuss Caribbean news, politics and culture – and, crucially, to discuss ways forward for Caribbean lives in Britain.

Published from a small office above a record shop in Brixton, the homeland of South London's Black community, the *West Indian Gazette* was an instant hit. Its first edition swiftly sold out, and the *Gazette* soon became a thriving and valued communication for the Caribbean community in Britain, bringing lively topical debate and incisive political comment to eager readers.

In Notting Hill, West London, Caribbean families had been settling for years. Black families lived alongside working-class white families in an area where landlords charged extortionate rent for cramped and overcrowded housing. But when Fascist groups began stirring up racial tensions in the area, Caribbean families came under attack from local white youths. These violent attacks persisted unchecked until Black residents fought back in the summer of 1958. The resulting clashes became known as the Notting Hill Riots.

How would people unite in the wake of such violence and unrest? Claudia was determined to demonstrate that Caribbean people were here to stay. The rich, glorious culture they had brought with them should be valued and celebrated: more than that, it could be the key to unity that would heal the community.

Trinidad, Claudia's home island, was home to the celebration known as Carnival. Every year, people parade the streets in colourful costume, dancing to the steel pan band, singing and swinging to calypso, cooking and sharing delicious dishes in an exuberant expression of joy, unity and community.

Claudia and her committee organised a Caribbean cultural celebration at St Pancras Town Hall in 1958 to coincide with Carnival in Trinidad. The team even had real palm trees brought from the Botanical Gardens at Kew!

The first five London 'Carnivals' would take place in indoor concert venues, but soon the Notting Hill Carnival became a street event more akin to the Trinidadian carnival that inspired it. Now Notting Hill Carnival is Europe's largest celebration of Caribbean culture.

Working year in year out, battling with the stresses of the struggles to change racially hostile political policy in Britain, took its toll on Claudia's health. In 1964, she died at her home in Gospel Oak, North London, aged just forty-nine. Claudia's ashes were buried in Highgate Cemetery, close to the grave of Karl Marx, the political thinker whose Communist beliefs and writings had so powerfully influenced her politics.

Claudia Jones's clarity of political vision and commitment to social justice were unwavering. Her idea to bring Caribbean culture centre stage transformed perceptions of Caribbeans in Britain. The immeasurable influence of Caribbean music, art and dance – the Carnival arts – continues to enrich and enliven British cultural life, decades after her death.

'A people's art is the genesis of their freedom'

GLOSSARY

ABOLITION the act of officially ending or getting rid of a system, practice or institution, such as the abolition of slavery

ACTIVIST a person who works to bring about social or political change through direct action, such as campaigning or protesting

CIVIL RIGHTS people's rights to fair treatment and equal opportunity, including the right to vote and freedom of expression

COLONISATION a system of oppression that begins with the act of taking over another country or region, usually by force, with the intention of replacing the existing systems, values and attitudes of the colonised country

COLONY a country or region that has been taken over by another country, usually by force

COMMUNIST a person who supports or believes in the principles of communism: a political and economic movement or government centred around the idea that wealth and resources should be shared out equally across the whole of society

EMANCIPATION the act of freeing people from enslavement

EMPIRE a group of nations that have been invaded and ruled over by another country

FASCISM a political movement or form of government based on far-right politics, characterised by extreme nationalism, racism and violent discrimination against multiple minority groups

FEMINIST a person who works to advance and protect the rights of women and girls, with the aim of establishing gender equality for all

GRASSROOTS POLITICS the actions of people at a local level, working to influence a political outcome

INDUSTRIALISATION a period of economic and social change, where machinery begins to be used to do work once done by people

LOBBYISTS people who try to persuade or influence members of a government or council to do something, such as change or abolish an existing law

MANUMISSION the granting of freedom to an enslaved individual

MIDDLE PASSAGE the second stage in the triangular journey of the transatlantic slave trade, in which African people were forcibly taken to the Americas in the holds of ships, in appalling conditions

PATOIS a spoken form of language or dialect, particular to a certain region, e.g., Jamaican patois

RACIAL DISCRIMINATION the act of treating someone differently or unfairly on the grounds of race, particularly in public services such as education, healthcare, employment or public transport

SEXISM prejudice or discrimination based on sex or gender, typically against women

SOCIAL JUSTICE the fair treatment of all people in society, where everyone should be given equal access to rights and opportunities

STRUCTURAL RACISM the laws, rules or policies that combine to perpetuate less visible forms of racial discrimination

BIBLIOGRAPHY

OVERVIEW

Edwards, Paul, and David Dabydeen (eds). *Black Writers in Britain 1760–1890*. Edinburgh: Edinburgh University Press, 1991.

Fryer, Peter. *Staying Power: The History of Black People in Britain*. London: Pluto Press, 1984.

Gerzina, Gretchen. *Black England: A Forgotten Georgian History*. London: John Murray, 2022.

Olusoga, David. *Black and British: A Forgotten History*. London: Macmillan, 2016.

Olusoga, David. *Black and British: A Short, Essential History*. London: Macmillan, 2020.

JOHN BLANKE

Kaufmann, Miranda. *Black Tudors: The Untold Story*. London: Oneworld, 2017.

Ohajuru, Michael. 'The John Blanke Project: Imagine the Black Tudor Trumpeter': https://www.johnblanke.com/, last accessed 24 January 2023.

IGNATIUS SANCHO

Carretta, Vincent. 'Sancho, (Charles) Ignatius (1729?–1780), author'. Oxford Dictionary of National Biography: https://www.oxforddnb.com/, last accessed 17 December 2022.

Carretta, Vincent (ed.). *Letters of the Late Ignatius Sancho, an African*. Toronto: Broadview Press, 2015.

Joseph, Paterson. *Sancho: An Act of Remembrance*. London: Oberon Books, 2011.

King, Reyahn, et al. *Ignatius Sancho: An African Man of Letters*. London: National Portrait Gallery, 1997.

OLAUDAH EQUIANO

Carretta, Vincent (ed.). *Olaudah Equiano: The Interesting Narrative and Other Writings*. New York: Penguin Group, 2003.

Edwards, Paul (ed.). *The Life of Olaudah Equiano*. Harlow: Longman, 1988.

Equiano, Olaudah. *The Interesting Narrative of the Life of Olaudah Equiano* (foreword by David Olusoga). London: Hodder & Stoughton, 2021.

Lovejoy, Paul E., et al. 'Equiano's World': www.equianosworld.org, last accessed 17 December 2022.

Osborne, Angelina. *Equiano's Daughter: The Life and Times of Joanna Vassa*. London: Krik Krak, 2007.

DIDO ELIZABETH BELLE

Byrne, Paula. *Belle: The True Story of Dido Belle*. London: William Collins, 2014.

Gerzina, Gretchen H. 'The Georgian Life and Modern Afterlife of Dido Elizabeth Belle', in *Britain's Black Past*, ed. Gretchen H. Gerzina. Liverpool: Liverpool University Press, 2020.

Major, Joanne, and Sarah Murden. 'All Things Georgian': https://georgianera.wordpress.com/, last accessed 24 January 2023.

MARY PRINCE

Ferguson, Moira. 'Prince [married name James], Mary (b. c. 1788), freed slave'. Oxford Dictionary of National Biography: https://www.oxforddnb.com/, last accessed 18 December 2022.

Maddison-MacFadyen, Margôt. 'Mary Prince': https://www.maryprince.org/, last accessed 18 December 2022.

Prince, Mary. *The History of Mary Prince, a West Indian Slave* (ed. Sara Salih). London: Penguin Classics, 2005.

MARY SEACOLE

Palmer, Alan. 'Seacole [née Grant], Mary Jane (1805–1881), nurse, doctress, and businesswoman'. Oxford Dictionary of National Biography: https://www.oxforddnb.com/, last accessed 18 December 2022.

Rappaport, Helen. *In Search of Mary Seacole: The Making of a Cultural Icon*. London: Simon & Schuster, 2022.

Seacole, Mary. *Wonderful Adventures of Mrs Seacole in Many Lands* (ed. Sara Salih). London: Penguin Classics, 2005.

IRA ALDRIDGE

Holder, Heidi J. 'Aldridge, Ira Frederick (1807?–1867), actor'. Oxford Dictionary of National Biography: https://www.oxforddnb.com/, last accessed 18 December 2022.

Hoyles, Martin. *Ira Aldridge: Celebrated 19th Century Actor*. London: Hansib, 2008.

Saxon, Theresa. 'Ira Aldridge in the North of England: Provincial Theatre and the Politics of Abolition', in *Britain's Black Past*, ed. Gretchen H. Gerzina. Liverpool: Liverpool University Press, 2020.

OMOBA AINA (SARAH FORBES BONETTA)

Anim-Addo, Joan. 'Bonetta [married name Davies], (Ina) Sarah Forbes [Sally] (c. 1843–1880), Queen Victoria's ward'. Oxford Dictionary of National Biography: https://www.oxforddnb.com/, last accessed 18 December 2022.

Anim-Addo, Joan. 'Queen Victoria's Black "Daughter"', in *Black Victorians / Black Victoriana*, ed. Gretchen Holbrook Gerzina. New Jersey: Rutgers University Press, 2003.

Bressey, Caroline. 'Of Africa's brightest ornaments: a short biography of Sarah Forbes Bonetta'. *Social & Cultural Geography*, Vol. 6, No. 2, 2005: 253–66.

Myers, Walter Dean. *At Her Majesty's Request: An African Princess in Victorian England*. New York: Scholastic Press, 1999.

SAMUEL COLERIDGE-TAYLOR

Bourne, Stephen. *Black Poppies: Britain's Black Community and the Great War*. Stroud: The History Press, 2014.

Green, Jeffrey. 'Samuel Coleridge-Taylor: Composer': https://jeffreygreen.co.uk/samuel-coleridge-taylor-composer/, last accessed 23 January 2023.

HAROLD MOODY

Bourne, Stephen. *Black Poppies: Britain's Black Community and the Great War*. Stroud: The History Press, 2014.

Killingray, David. 'Moody, Harold Arundel (1882–1947), physician and founder of the League of Coloured Peoples'. Oxford Dictionary of National Biography: https://www.oxforddnb.com/, last accessed 18 December 2022.

Schwarz, Bill (ed.). *West Indian Intellectuals in Britain*. Manchester: Manchester University Press, 2003.

WALTER TULL

Barbados Museum & Historical Society. 'Walter Tull: A Strong Heart Beating Loudly': https://waltertullexhibition.org/, last accessed 17 December 2022.

Bourne, Stephen. *Black Poppies: Britain's Black Community and the Great War*. Stroud: The History Press, 2014.

Daniel, Peter, and Phil Vasili. *Crossing the White Line: The Walter Tull Story. KS2 Activity Pack*. Westminster Archives: https://www.wwiplayingthegame.org.uk, last accessed 23 January 2023.

Olusoga, David. *The World's War: Forgotten Soldiers of Empire*. London: Head of Zeus, 2015.

Vasili, Phil. 'Tull, Walter Daniel John (1888–1918), footballer and army officer'. Oxford Dictionary of National Biography: https://www.oxforddnb.com/, last accessed 17 December 2022.

EVELYN DOVE

Bourne, Stephen. *Black Poppies: Britain's Black Community and the Great War*. Stroud: The History Press, 2014.

Bourne, Stephen. *Evelyn Dove: Britain's Black Cabaret Queen*. London: Jacaranda, 2016.

Parsonage, Catherine. *The Evolution of Jazz in Britain, 1880–1935*. Aldershot: Ashgate, 2005.

UNA MARSON

Donnell, Alison (ed.). *Una Marson: Selected Poems*. Leeds: Peepal Tree Press, 2011.

Jarrett-Macauley, Delia. *The Life of Una Marson 1905–65*. Manchester: Manchester University Press, 1998.

Osborne, Dr Deirdre. 'An introduction to Una Marson's poetry'. Discovering Literature, British Library: https://www.bl.uk/20th-century-literature/articles/an-introduction-to-una-marsons-poetry, last accessed 23 January 2023.

'Una Marson'. Discovering Literature, British Library: https://www.bl.uk/people/una-marson, last accessed 23 January 2023.

CLAUDIA JONES

Courtman, Sandra. 'Claudia Jones' rebel heart'. Windrush Stories, British Library: https://www.bl.uk/windrush/articles/claudia-jones-rebel-heart, last accessed 23 January 2023.

Sherwood, Marika. *Claudia Jones: A Life in Exile*. London: Lawrence & Wishart, 1999.

A NOTE ON LANGUAGE
In this book we have used the word Black with a capital B to denote people of African or African Caribbean descent. The language we use to talk about race changes over time. Even the idea of 'race' itself is not something fixed, but something that has been invented to categorise people artificially. We hope that this book will inspire you to discuss these histories and to carry out your own research.

NOTES ON THE QUOTATIONS
p. 25: Letter from Ignatius Sancho to Julius Soubise, November 1778.

p. 27: Letter from Ignatius Sancho to Mr M---, November 1772.

p. 31: Letter from Ignatius Sancho to William Stevenson, April 1779.

pp. 35, 37 and 38: *The Interesting Narrative of the Life of Olaudah Equiano*, 1789.

p. 47: *The London Chronicle*, 1788.

p. 55: *The History of Mary Prince, a West Indian Slave, related by Herself*, 1831.

pp. 66 and 72: *Wonderful Adventures of Mrs Seacole in Many Lands*, 1857.

p. 80: Ira Aldridge's Announcement on becoming Theatre Manager, Coventry, 1828.

p. 87: Letter from Captain Forbes to the Secretary of the Admiralty, 1850.

p. 97: Song from *The Song of Hiawatha* by Samuel Coleridge-Taylor.

p. 101: Inscription on a silver cup given to Samuel Coleridge-Taylor in America.

p. 120: *Football Star*, March 1909.

p. 132: *Evening News of India*, 7 October 1937.

p. 155: Claudia Jones, First London Carnival Programme, January 1959

ABOUT THE AUTHOR AND ILLUSTRATOR
Joanna Brown writes for children as J.T. Williams to illuminate the lives and literature, the stories and histories of Black people in Britain. She studied English Literature at the University of Cambridge before becoming a primary school teacher. J.T. Williams is the author of *The Lizzie and Belle Mysteries*, an award-winning historical mystery series set in Georgian London.

Angela Vives is an illustrator with a Master's in children's book illustration from the Cambridge School of Art at Anglia Ruskin University. In 2021 she won the Picture Hooks Winter Comforts competition, and was Highly Commended for Faber's FAB Prize and for The Macmillan Prize in illustration. Prior to being a children's illustrator, Angela was a video editor working in the advertising industry in London. She grew up in Colombia.

ACKNOWLEDGEMENTS
No book is the work of one person alone. I would like to thank: Anna Ridley, our constant champion at Thames & Hudson, for her passion, vision and support; Izzie Hewitt for her sunny smile and for the wisdom and warmth of her editorial direction; Kate Haynes and Avni Patel for the spectacular creative flair of their art direction; and Jenny Wilson for her sensitive and steady hand, and her unerringly incisive editorial eye. Profound thanks to my dear friend Angela Vives for her sublime illustrations, for the heart and soul given so that this book could sing through pictures as well as words.

INDEX